YOSEF AND MARYAM

Written by
MARTIN BARON

DEDICATION

This work is dedicated to my two lovely daughters Kristina and Lara, the Loves of my life. Also to my late father and especially to my mother who prayed so hard to St Joseph for me to be born on his feast-day, the 19th of March. I made it by only five minutes to spare. It is dedicated also to Sandra who was always there to encourage me from start to finish with Love. And to my late uncle Joseph, who was always full of gratitude for what he had, and like the Saint he was named for, never stopped loving.

It is also dedicated to the many others in my life who loved me, often more than I deserved.

Love is truly its own reward.

YOSEF AND MARYAM

MARTIN BARON

YOSEF
AND
MARYAM

YOSEF AND MARYAM

CHAPTER ONE

"You can't see her ... Yosef, sorry ... she's not well ... maybe later ..."

Yosef grimaced. It had been the third morning in a row that Hannah, his mother-in-law to be, had denied him a visit to his betrothed and beloved Maryam.

But this time round, he noticed something different in Hannah's eyes: they couldn't look directly into his. He tugged nervously at his thick black curls. *Why? Is she hiding something?* He wondered—could she be lying? Could Maryam be in a really bad state and not just have an upset stomach, after all? What stomach stays upset for a whole week?

Could Maryam even be dead?

"I demand to see her!" he yelled, alarmed at this last thought.

Hannah took two steps backwards and almost tripped over her doorstep. Yosef was a heavily built man, and his voice was as powerful as his physique. She was a tall woman too, but no match for him.

"You ... you cannot! She is not dressed; she is in bed. It ... it isn't proper ..." stammered Hannah, seemingly at the point of tears.

"I shall not move from this doorway till I see her!" Yosef felt his anger mounting. "Where's Yehoyaqim? I demand he gives me permission!"

"My husband is at the Synagogue! Go! Go and ask him there." Hannah tried to shoo him off.

Yosef's eyes narrowed. He knew very well this was a ruse. No one would dare interrupt Yehoyaqim at his daily prayers, maybe not even the priest himself. He felt about to explode, yet his voice came out low and icy, "I do not like this! I do not like this at all! And I do not believe what you are saying. There is something wrong, and I sense it." He then made a sudden lunge and almost succeeded in shoving her inside.

Yet, although thin and frail, Hannah blocked his way valiantly and started to push ineffectively at his wide chest with both hands. She might as well have pushed against a brick wall.

"You stop right there or I shall scream and bring out the whole neighbourhood!" she threatened, alarmed.

Already, they could hear the creaking of shutters, indicating that the scene they were making had not altogether gone unnoticed. One shutter finally swung open with a loud creak. However, it was right above, at Hannah's own house.

A decidedly green face looked down at him timidly. *Maryam*

"Hey, Yosef! Calm down, will you? I'm alright, don't worry. Just a bit weak, alright? I've just been throwing up again."

Yosef's eyes fixed on the figure leaning out of the tiny window. At finally seeing his beloved, he breathed a sigh of relief; and then his eyes misted over at noticing the state of her face, barely visible under a shock of dishevelled hair which was as black as coal.

"Are you really alright?" he asked in a weak, broken voice, and one which he didn't like at all. He promptly gave a cough to clear it. Soft and imploring, his eyes looked steadily upwards from under bushy eyebrows which were drawn together in concern.

"Yes I am." Maryam smiled bravely back down at him. "Do be patient, my love. I will soon get better ... maybe this evening ... we shall come over.

For, although formally betrothed for several months now, the two were never permitted to be alone together.

"You should go and see Baruch again ..." Yosef started.

Maryam stared down at him, blinked, bit her lower lip, and said nothing. Yosef turned to Hannah, his anger rising again.

"She *has* been to see Baruch?"

Hannah's confounded silence gave him his answer.

Yosef put his large face right up to hers. "Why are you so stubborn?" he yelled, "sick for a whole week and you did not even send for the physician? How do you expect her to get well? By prayers alone?" There was more than a hint of sarcasm in his voice. "Or is it the money? She could have something serious ..."

A shutter opened overhead and the face of an old woman stared down at them from a high window across the alley.

Now it was Hannah's turn to get angry. She went white in the face.

"Yosef! Go away right now!" she hissed. "We cannot continue arguing in the street like this. You have seen her now! If she is better, and *only* if she is better, this evening we might come over to your house! That's it!"

She took a step backwards and slammed the door in his face. Yosef could not believe it. He kept his gaze fixed on the door and then looked up just in time to see Maryam being yanked back from the windowsill by her mother. The shutter was slammed shut. He then turned to the other window; the one which still sported old Ribqah's deeply wrinkled face. She grinned toothlessly down at him.

Her unashamedly intrusive attention to their situation was what stopped him from kicking the door in. He gave a furious grunt, then tramped off in disgust.

YOSEF AND MARYAM

CHAPTER TWO

"Maryam!"

"Maryam!" Diynah shouted again, this time even louder.

But Maryam did not hear, or maybe she heard, and did not heed. She was sitting with a large group of children on the cool limestone paving of the school courtyard. Her delicate mouth hung open, as she sat transfixed by the theatrics of Shimon, a gangly, pale-faced man in his mid-twenties, who was strutting up and down on a makeshift stage at the end of the courtyard. Maryam was right up in the front-row, with the other children. Not that she was much of a child any longer. Always taller than anyone of her age by far, her recent coming of age had added so much to her height that she now fairly towered above the rest, even whilst sitting down. Shimon could hardly keep his eyes off her. Her thick, tall and silky black hair hung in large ringlets down to her shoulders. Her face was ivory-skinned, and two large dark-brown eyes were exquisitely set wide apart in it like matching jewels.

Shimon was pacing back and forth on the stage.

He continued, "So old Auntie Rachel came to visit and brought two red apples as gifts for the children: for Debora and little Solomo. She placed them on the kitchen table. 'These are for you, my lovelies, she told them,' then went into the courtyard to help their mama hang out the clothes to dry.

"The two children were alone now. And they both looked excitedly at the two apples. They were dark red: their favourite type!

One problem, though," he paused.

His audience looked up, eyes widening in expectation.

"One of the apples was twice as big as the other!"

Peals of laughter rang out from the group.

"Well, so what happens next?" This time Shimon's pause was shorter.

"Well, little Solomo immediately grabs the bigger apple and takes a huge bite at it."

All the children laughed and quite a few clapped in merriment.

"So his sister Debora shouts out, 'hey Solomo ... stop! Stop it! Don't you dare eat that apple! That is very rude, you know?!'"

Shimon had raised his already shrill voice even higher and the children screamed in delight. He removed the hand he placed firmly on his hips to wag an accusatory finger at the imaginary Solomo. He then puffed out his cheeks to make them appear as though filled with apple, and gobbled out Solomo's reply,

'What's rude?'

'Well, young man! You should not have grabbed the large one just like that and started gobbling it!'"

"Maryam!" Diynah was fairly screaming now.

Maryam finally looked behind her, and seeing her friend, tried to wave her off impatiently.

Shimon noticed Diynah and gave her a frown. He resumed,

"Well, children, Solomo gulped down his mouthful of apple, and with a mischievous look on his face replied, 'well, what would *you* have done instead, sweet dear sister of mine?'

"'Well, I, I,'" Shimon emphatically jabbed with his index finger at his chest with his every 'I', "'I would instead have chosen the smaller apple and offered the larger one to you!' she replied."

Again, Shimon wagged his index finger vigorously down at the imaginary little Solomo.

"'Great!' replies Solomo and he calmly reaches out, picks up the little apple off the table and hands it over to her, saying, 'Why, that's exactly like it is right now: you have the little one and I have the big one. Happy? So why all the fuss?'"

Shimon clapped his hands together, grinned and waited for the response of his audience.

It took a moment to sink in, and when it did the group of children gave a scream, jumped to their feet, laughing, clapping and cheering. Maryam also shrieked with laughter and rocked back and forth on the ground, holding her tall slender belly with both hands.

Shimon was visibly pleased at the success of his tale, and was comically taking enormous, profuse bows.

Maryam then noticed him eagerly seeking her eyes—perhaps for a more personalised approval—but she was suddenly yanked her to her feet by Diynah and pulled away from the cheering crowd. She didn't fail to also notice however how his face fell before she turned away to go. Maryam felt his eyes bore into her back as they weaved their way through the jumping and yelling crowd, in the direction of the arched doorway.

"Ha ha ha!" Maryam was faltering in her steps, halting, bending over and laughing. She stopped and held on to the side of the stone arch with one hand.

"Come on, come *on*, we're late, the others are waiting for us!" urged Diynah, tugging her out to the street.

"That Shimon is so, so funny. He'll be the death of me," Maryam said with tears in her eyes.

"Yes, very witty, I'm sure," Diynah replied impatiently. "We all know that, now come *on!"*

****

The two teenage girls, their long, voluminous skirts hitched clear of their ankles, rushed through the busy village of Nazaret. Turning a corner sharply, without pausing to look, Maryam suddenly bumped head to head into a sleepy-looking grey donkey, which was drawing a small cart laden with vegetables. The donkey brayed, nostrils flaring wide, and reared up on its hind legs. Maryam screamed first in surprise, then in fear, as its two flailing hooves barely missed her head. She shrieked with laughter at the situation, to be yanked forward once more by Diynah. The donkey reared up again at the sound of her laughter, this time even higher.

They raced away. Maryam, hearing a yell, chanced a backward glance. The farmer, who had been walking, or rather limping, behind the cart had been bowled over by an avalanche of cabbages, cob-corn, and cauliflowers off the upended cart. He angrily swept himself clear of the load, swiftly leapt back to his feet and gave chase after them, flourishing his whip. Giggling, Maryam and Diynah twisted and turned, swerved and doubled back in the maze of alleys of Nazaret, and they soon managed to lose him. Finally, breathing heavily, they slowed down, and warily crept up to the large old house which stood at the end of a narrow, shady alley; the house where their friend Marta lived. Diynah placed her finger to her lips and Maryam stopped giggling.

Diynah gently lifted the door latch. "Grandmother Esther is taking a nap under the stairs!" she whispered to Maryam, who gave her a silent nod, and the two stepped gingerly inside. Lifting their heavy skirts, they tiptoed up the wide stone staircase. Halfway up, a loud snore practically shook the steps under their feet. Maryam clapped a hand to her mouth to stifle her laughter as Diynah hissed, eyes flashing at her their dire warning.

At the top of the stairs they came to a landing and Diynah gently opened the door to the roof above the house. A blast of hot afternoon air welcomed them as they walked across the flat blue-tiled rooftop.

In one corner, a group of three other girls crouched together under the walled perimeter, which was some three feet high, taking turns to cautiously peer over it.

And they were all silently giggling. The two newcomers walked towards them.

"Is he still there?" Diynah asked Marta, her voice barely above a whisper, as she stopped Maryam from coming too close to the wall.

"Yes," Marta, turning her head, whispered back.

Maryam and Diynah crouched down, and shuffled over to the low border of the rooftop.

"Maryam!" Marta hissed, "Crouch lower! You're too tall. One at a time now, we're all taking turns."

One of the other girls giggled. Diynah peered over the wall and smiled. Maryam crouched beside her and when her turn came, she gently raised her head so she could look over the wall.

She looked over and down onto the alley. On the other side of it, a cat slept soundly on a shady window sill. The world was quiet, with the exception of one place ... Her eyes intent, she travelled them to the workshop right across.

Outside its wide doorway, large planks of wood were stacked

on one side and huge logs on the other. The weather-beaten door was closed, but from their vantage point the girls could look right through a cross-barred, high window onto the workshop floor inside.

A bearded, heavy-set young man was sawing a log into sections. His exertions had turned his face bright red and sweat poured profusely over his brow. He paused to wipe it off with a muscular arm; an arm drenched with sweat and peppered with sawdust.

And he had no shirt on.

Maryam stared and felt her face flush with heat. She had never seen a man with his shirt off before. Not even her father. And what a man this was! The girls giggled behind her and prodded her for attention. But she could not pull her eyes away. After a while, the carpenter stopped and lifted what remained of the heavy log off the rack. With a heave, he stood it against the wall. His biceps seemed to double in size with the effort.

Maryam gasped.

Upon hearing it, the other girls did not wait for their turn but peered over the roof in unison.

Maryam then felt a sudden pang of shame; still hot in the face, she dipped back below the low wall.

The carpenter stopped and started to turn round, whereupon the row of heads on the wall disappeared behind it in a flash.

The girls sat with their backs to the wall. Maryam's thighs fairly baked with the heat radiating up from the rooftop. All the girls were very red in the face, and they knew very well that the afternoon sun was not the sole cause of it.

Maryam's heart beat fast. She placed a hand on her chest, as if to calm it down. The other girls saw this and sniggered.

"Do you come and watch every day?" she finally asked Marta with bated breath, stunned.

"No," giggled Marta, "not *every* day!" The others laughed.

"What if Papa catches you?" asked Maryam in wonder.

"Well, he would kill me for sure!"

"Or make you marry him, Marta!" laughed Diynah.

Maryam felt a sudden pang of jealousy at the prospect.

She then shrugged it off. After all, her eyes were set on the other carpenter of the village.

'But then ... Yosef is twice as big and twice as handsome,' she thought. And it had not been the first time he had caught her eye, especially with those light brown eyes of his peering through his bushy eyebrows. And although she could practically remember every single time she had met him, she had never seen him this way before—what these last brief moments had made her feel, she had never ever felt before, for any man.

She supposed now that she was a woman; she would mostly feel this way towards most men. She felt somewhat confused and resolved that she was still growing up and had a lot left to learn. Maybe her friends would teach her. For, of course, she could only ever have one man, one husband. And not only that, but most likely, one had to be chosen for her. She really could not very well choose him for herself, although she had long ago made up her mind to, at the very least, let her mother know of her preference.

Marta gingerly peered again over the wall. "He's gone! The door's open but the place is empty," she whispered to the others.

Their faces fell.

"Well ... till the next time then, come on girls," she said, with a tone of resignation.

The girls shuffled low across the baking tiles until they were at a safe distance from the wall on the roof, just in case. They then stood straight and crept softly down the stairs.

CHAPTER THREE

Maryam opened her door to answer a knock so soft, she wasn't really sure she'd heard it at all. Beyond the threshold stood Shimon, very red in the face and peering back up the alley over his shoulder. He was holding a package in his hand. His head snapped back and he gave her a nervous smile.

"Hi Shimon, what's up? Do you want Papa? He's not in."

Shimon gave a nervous shake to his eagle-like head.

"Is it Mama then? Well, she's not here either; they both left together for Hebron. They're visiting some relatives. Auntie Shelomit will be back from the market soon."

"I ... I ... it is you I came to see, Maryam,"

Shimon was visibly agitated and a sheen of sweat glistened on his brow.

"Really?" Maryam tried to sound impressed, but she was not altogether surprised. "What on earth for?"

Shimon hesitated; he pursed his lips and then replied in a voice much firmer than his usual, "I need to speak with you. May ... May I come in? "

"Yes of course, go ahead Shimon, tell me, but ... you'd better stay out here, on the doorstep. There's no-one else at home, you know." Maryam felt a little flutter in her stomach.

Shimon nodded vigorously.

"Of course, of course," he said. "Maryam, I notice you always come over to the courtyard when I entertain the children after prayers at the school."

"Yes, Shimon, I do, it's true. I like it very much. You really make me laugh."

"But you are no longer a child ..."

"So, am I not allowed to laugh anymore?"

"Of course, of course you are," affirmed Shimon hastily.

"But ..." He hesitated for a moment, and then seemed to have wound up the courage to say what he wanted to say, "but is it me you like or just my jokes?"

Now it was Maryam's turn to hesitate; she knew where Shimon was heading.

"Well, the jokes would be flat, I think, should it be someone less capable telling them! Someone like me, for example."

She giggled at the mere thought. "So ..."

"So ...," he pressed on hopefully.

"So, I must like you too then, obviously." Then she added hastily, "I mean, I like *the way* you tell them."

"Oh!" said Shimon, his face falling.

"What's that?" Maryam pointed at the package he was nervously shifting from one hand to the other.

"This?" asked Shimon, giving a start. He seemed to have almost forgotten about it. "This ... this is something for you."

"For me? A gift? Oh! Really? Thank you Shimon, how sweet of you! What is it? Can I open it?"

"Eh? Not out here! In the middle of the street. Can't we go inside?"

"What?" Maryam almost shouted. "Of course not! I told you. There's no one else at home. It is not proper."

"Sorry, I'm sorry," Shimon said hastily. "I should not have asked. It's just that I don't like people prying." He raised an eyebrow and nodded over to his left. Maryam leaned out and looked up to see old Ribqah at her window, watching them.

"Oh, don't mind her," Maryam re-assured him, "why, she would know everything anyway. He he he!"

"Go on then, open it!" Shimon eagerly handed her the package.

Maryam quickly loosened the neatly tied twine and removed the cloth.

"A jewellery box!" she exclaimed. "Why, it's beautiful ... inlaid too!"

She turned it round and round in her pale, slender-fingered hands and tried to undo the shiny brass latch. Thin blue veins snaked through the delicate skin of the back of her hand. It was closed tight.

"How do you open it, Shimon?"

"Eh, hold on now, Maryam, one moment! I have to tell you something first: the box, well, the box is empty ..."

Maryam paused and then gave a sharp burst of laughter.

"Ha ha ha! But of course it is, Shimon, ha ha ha! I just wanted to see how it is lined inside. You can't stop joking for one moment now, can you?"

"I wasn't joking," Shimon said gravely.

"What do you mean?" Maryam looked at him, confused. She then added, "What I meant was, I did not expect to find anything inside!"

"There *is* nothing inside," Shimon affirmed seriously, then went on, "for now at least!"

Maryam looked at him searchingly.

"Shimon! What has gotten into you? Of course I expected to find nothing inside. Why, I did not even expect this box."

She tried again to undo the latch, to no avail. "It is beautiful," she repeated. "Thank you ... thank you very much."

Then her brow furrowed briefly, and she asked him, "Shimon, what did you mean by '*for now*'?"

Shimon stretched out to his full height and solemnly declared, "Maryam, I am prepared to start filling that box for you with silver, gold and precious stones!"

Maryam's jaw dropped. Eyes wide, she found it difficult to speak. Heat pricked at her cheeks.

"I asked you whether you liked me," he went on, "and you said '*yes*'. Well, I too like you very much."

Then he declared, "And out of all the pretty maidens in the village it is *your* hand I wish to ask for!"

Maryam gave a start and dropped the box. It bounced off the paving and the lid flew open. Its shining silk lining, coloured ruby red, could now be seen. It also had a mirror inside the lid, which somehow had not been broken in the fall.

"Oh!" Maryam gasped in dismay. She grabbed the box back up off the ground.

"Sorry Shimon, I ... I didn't mean to drop it!" She dusted it off and, heart pounding, examined it for damage. One brass hinge was a little loose.

Shimon looked on, crestfallen, but said nothing. He looked at her expectantly as she scrutinised the box for more damage, while she thought hard of how to reply. From the corner of her eye, she spotted a thin sheen of sweat re-appear on his brow.

"Shimon, I am too young ..." she started, as she looked at the ground, her voice barely above a whisper.

"You are not, Maryam! I know full well you are already thirteen."

"But Shimon, I do not *want* to get married, not even betrothed, for now at least. I like being a child ..."

"But you are not a child, Maryam, not anymore!" Shimon said scathingly. "Look at me!"

Maryam slowly raised her eyes to meet his.

"I mean what I said about that jewellery box: as my wife I will respect you and make you happy, and not just with gifts and things. Few others in the village have my position, my means."

"A carpenter!" Maryam teased him. For although Shimon's sudden proposition had come as a shock, she was inwardly pleased to see him insisting, glad that he wanted her so much.

"Yes, *a carpenter*, true. But a very wealthy and renowned one, as you must certainly know." Shimon's voice now had a distinct edge to it.

"There is more than *one* carpenter in the village, Shimon," Maryam replied mysteriously.

Shimon looked stunned. He glared at her, as the colour drained from his flushed face.

"What? Who? Yosef? Come on ... *carpenter*? All he basically does is saw wood all day long, or maybe construct a clunky cabinet or two from time to time," he scoffed. Then he pointedly added, "whereas, I—*I*—sell my furniture to the very rich, to high quality clients."

He tapped with his index finger at on the jewellery box Maryam was holding with both hands.

"Even to King Herod himself! And, have you seen my doors? The wood is as smooth as silk; the joints: hardly visible; the fittings: perfect. Why, you'd almost hesitate to knock on them.

Now, as for the doors made by Yosef, those make you want to bang hard on them, maybe even kick them."

He gave a short laugh, "more suitable for some shed I'd say."

He glanced over Maryam's shoulder, "why, like that one, in fact!" He pointed at Maryam's own rugged, nondescript door, and then dropped his arm as he quickly realised his mistake.

"Well, I like that!" Maryam yelled at him, hands on her hips, offended. "For your information, that is the only door we can afford, Shimon, and though it may not be *as smooth as silk*, as you put it, it is solid and serves its purpose well. We do not live in a mansion," she added, raising her eyebrows as far as they could go, "as everyone can clearly see!"

"But you see, Maryam, you could! You *could* live in a mansion. You only need to say, *'Yes'.*" Don't you see what I am offering you? A life of comfort, security: of happiness."

Maryam was confused at his words, and it must have showed on her face, and this seemed to encourage him. He continued, "Aren't you happy when you laugh?"

She nodded, bemused.

"See?" he said with a smile. "So I make you happy almost every day already. There!"

"That is true," she replied firmly.

She gathered her thoughts for a moment, then said in a serious tone, "yes, true, but life is not only about laughter: there is a lot of hard work and a lot of pain and sorrow in it, too."

"So?" he countered. "Who can you find who can protect you best from sorrow, or at least try to make up for it, maybe give some meaning to it? At the very least my sense of humour can definitely alleviate the pain a bit."

"Shimon." Maryam shifted tack. "You are too short for me!"

Shimon was visibly taken aback at this and inadvertently straightened up.

"Well, Maryam. That is not exactly correct; I'll have you know. It is *you* who are too tall for me! You are the tallest girl in the village!" He smiled at his own wit, and then added graciously, "and although you have the height of a man, I still prefer you!"

"I don't feel comfortable about it, Shimon!" Maryam insisted. "We'd look funny walking down the street and all!"

"Well, it doesn't bother me, and I'm the one who should really be bothered, am I not? And furthermore, Maryam, let me tell you, you practically have no choice! Don't you see? No man is taller than you are over here, in Nazaret, I mean. Now maybe in Yerushalayim, in Hebron, or in Kerios you could maybe find—"

Maryam raised her right palm, stopping him in mid-sentence.

"You're wrong Shimon. There is someone who is ..."

"Who?"

Maryam bit her lower lip and said nothing.

Shimon shook his head and pursed his lips in thought, then his eyes narrowed.

"You don't mean that Yosef again surely?"

Maryam assented with a slight and gentle nod, which infuriated Shimon.

"You must be joking!" he yelled angrily. "Yosef! My, what a match! He is much older than you are for a start. And he is barely taller than you, more like your height, I'd say. Whatever: he is uncouth and dirt poor!"

Shimon's voice was much too loud.

Maryam glanced up and down the alley nervously. But except for a scrawny black cat busy licking at its paw in a patch of sunshine in the corner, the alley was deserted.

"He is not much older than me and he is *not* dirt poor," she then retorted indignantly. "Well, not as rich as you are, for sure. Also, he may not be at all wealthy, but at least he is of the house of Dawid, as is my family."

Shimon looked at her. His eyes had darkened at being reminded that he, on the contrary, was not.

"Maybe, that may be so, but whatever his family line, nonetheless he is still a mindless clod! *Come on!* Maryam, be sensible! What do you want your life to be, one of sweeping away sawdust for him all day long, or rather one where you get to order your handmaiden around?

"As I said, Yosef is basically a woodcutter, a glorified lumberjack. He cannot keep you in comfort. You'd practically starve! He also only sells locally and does repairs. He does not sell to the wealthy, to the King ..."

"To the Romans ..." Maryam's sudden dark interjection stopped Shimon in his tracks.

Shimon's face had lost its last vestige of colour. He gritted his teeth, wrung his bony white hands, and tapped his foot nervously. Maryam felt certain that he was fully aware of the resentment many people at the village felt at his well-known selling to the much-hated, occupying enemy.

"So what?" he countered furiously. "If *I* did not sell to the Romans, someone else would! It's as simple as that! What is wrong with keeping money in our community? Taking back a part of the taxes they fleece off us? Would you rather have them buy from the Samaritans? Or even from the Philistines? What's wrong with selling them a bit of furniture, a door or a window, here and there?"

"But you also sell them *crosses*!"

Maryam inhaled sharply. Amazed at herself for having spoken out so bluntly she could hardly believe her own courage.

Shimon's face had by now turned into an ashen grey. Through glistening red-rimmed eyes he glared at Maryam who, in turn, glowered back at him. His hand inadvertently towards the jewellery box, but he drew it back just in time, transforming the movement to a nervous wave.

His voice came out calm and cold. "Yes I know many stupid people here hold *that* against me. Someone *has* to sell them the crosses, don't you see? But know this, it is not *I* who condemn people to die on them! *I* have nothing to do with that! Nothing at all!"

"But Yosef does *not* sell them crosses!" said Maryam, almost adding *'even though he is dirt poor,'* and thinking the better of it.

Shimon looked devastated. His mouth opened and closed. For once he was speechless. Trembling in agitation, he finally sputtered, "wait just one minute here, do you seriously believe I could be contracted to supply the Romans with their every requirement and then choose to just *opt out* of the crosses? Why, they would immediately stop working with me! What would you have me do? Lose all that business for just a miserable cross now and again?

Maryam blushed but said nothing.

Shimon's eyes narrowed to slits, and he parried cynically, "and then have to accept jobs from the Leper Community instead, as *your* Yosef does?"

Maryam looked stunned. Shimon sneered in triumph.

"Well, that's most probably just a rumour," she said after a pause. "No-one would be *that* crazy."

Then she retorted angrily, "and ... he is not *my* Yosef."

"Well ... the way you speak of him, the way you defend him, he might just as well be." Shimon's voice was poignant now, and Maryam felt some dismay.

"Shimon, I have to think about this. Sorry, I did not mean to offend you, I really didn't, about the crosses, I mean ... I know you are not a bad man. I mean it." She tapped the back of his hand affectionately. Shimon looked only slightly relieved.

She quickly went on, "um, I wonder if you could fix this hinge for me. She fingered the loose hinge delicately. "I'm so sorry I dropped it."

 He gave a reluctant nod.

With a wistful look at the jewellery box, she handed it over, sensing somehow that she would not have it back again.

"Yes, of course, alright, alright, Maryam. I too am sorry. I should not have asked you outright, and so bluntly, for your hand. He walked off, then stopped and looked over his sunken shoulder at her, "so do think about it, will you? Please?"

Maryam nodded, ever so slightly.

He turned away again, gave a couple of faltering steps, then halted and looked once more back at her. "One more thing, Maryam ..."

He paused and took a deep breath as he turned to face her. "You do know that in these matters it is not for you to decide, don't you? I can always insist on asking your father for your hand. After all, we all know parents always do know what is best for their children, and for their family."

There was more than just a hint of condescension in his voice. Maryam tried to hide her disgust.

"Yes Shimon, I do know, of course," she replied flatly.

Shimon nodded again and tramped back down the street, his head hung low.

For the first time in her life, Maryam gave a good look at her door before going inside and closing it behind her.

CHAPTER FOUR

"Marta!"

"Yes, Mama?"

"We've practically run out of food again. So soon! Good God! How you have been eating lately my girl! Teenage appetite, I suppose," said Jessica eyeing her slim daughter quizzically. "Not much to show for it yet, though, eh?" she laughed.

Martha blushed and said nothing.

"So, my growing little lady, as you know, we need wheat, barley and lentils. And let me see ..., also we need beans, meat, dates, olives and, well, practically everything else. So I'd better be off to the market."

Marta's face lit up at these words and this didn't escape her mother's gimlet eyes, which also did not fail to notice that Marta was dressed in her fine 'outside' clothes.

"Ah, you dressed up to come with me? Well, come along then," Jessica told her.

"No, Mama, it's alright. You go, I'll stay here"

"What?" Jessica was nonplussed, for usually Marta took every opportunity to be out. "Well, alright then, have it your way, but don't laze about now, or go chasing after your friends!"

"No, I won't," replied Marta truthfully.

"Do the dishes."

"Yes, Mama."

"And sweep the floor."

"Yes, Mama."

"Of the whole house!"

"Yes, Mama."

"Why do you keep saying *"Yes"* to everything?" Her mother snapped at her.

"Why not? Should I say *"No"* instead?"

"No!"

"Yes, Mama."

Jessica raised her eyes to the ceiling and rolled them ostentatiously.

"May the good God deliver us from teenage girls!" She then gave a smile. "I'm off now, little lady. Be sure to do all those things I told you, mind!"

"Yes, Mama!" Marta grinned.

Jessica frowned, pulled her shawl close to her face, grabbed her huge wicker basket, stepped out, and slammed the door shut behind her.

Marta hesitated for the briefest of moments, then sped up the stairs to the flagstone paved-rooftop and watched as her mother strode down the alley and turned the corner. She then raced back down and made straight for a wooden kitchen stool, which was in its usual place, next to a large sink hewn out of a solid block of stone. She grabbed it and ran out into the courtyard. Marta then slammed the stool to the ground. It bounced off the limestone paving. She picked it up and examined it. *It was intact!* The girl puffed as she raised the heavy stool by its legs well over her head, to slam it back to the ground. It bounced off the paving, higher this time, with a clatter; still intact. Marta stood there, hands firm on her hips, glaring at the stool for some moments. She then picked it up once more, tossed it into the kitchen sink and poured a nearby bucket of water all over it. She waited for a moment, then fished it out and slammed it again to the floor with all the force she could muster. The stool bounced yet higher, but remained still very much intact. Marta screamed and hopped in anger. She grabbed hold of it by one of its three legs and climbed back up the stairs to the roof. Without even a pause, she hurled it down hard to the courtyard below. There was a large thud, followed by a scream. *Mama!*

"Oh God!" Marta gasped, her hand to her mouth. She rushed down the stairs and saw her mother at the doorway to the courtyard, holding a hand to her chest, panting heavily, and staring at the upended stool right in front of her. A stool that finally had one of its legs askew. Marta grinned. Her mother frowned, lunged forward and raised her hand to slap her daughter across the face; but just managed to stop it inches away. She shook it in her face instead.

"What in the blessed name of God do you think you're doing? Have you gone crazy?" she demanded, enraged.

"And, what were you doing up there?" Jessica jabbed her finger at the roof that gave onto the courtyard. "My God what a fright you gave me the moment I opened that door!"

"Um, Mama, I, well, why are you back so soon? Did you forget something?" she asked, obviously trying to gain time.

"You answer my question first, my girl!" Jessica yelled at her.

"I, um ... I took the stool up to the roof and it fell, of course."

"For God's sake, why on earth did you take the stool up to the roof? Not to sit around and bask in the sun, I hope? And, what about the chores?"

"Mama, listen, I'll explain. I ... was about to do the dishes and splashed water onto the stool, and I couldn't very well sit down on a wet stool, now could I, especially with these clothes on." Her delicate fingers rolled and pointed at her colourful skirt.

"So you took it up to the roof to dry," said her mother, trying to make some sense of the situation.

"Yes, that's it!"

"But why not down here, my dear? There is plenty of sun."

Jessica swept her arm over to a bright patch of sunlit tiles in the courtyard.

"Ah, yes," said Marta, thinking quickly, "but no wind, eh? It would have dried faster up there."

She pointed to the roof, grinning inwardly at her own ingenuity.

"Maybe, had you not managed to drop it," said her mother scathingly.

"Yes, sorry about that."

"And break it!"

"Yes, unfortunately." replied her daughter mischievously, then added, "but I'll have it fixed, don't fret, and right away!"

"We can't really afford to at the moment. We could use one of the oak chairs instead, from the kitchen."

"Oh, no! No need, we can easily have it fixed. The carpenter, he won't charge us much. Here ...," Marta stepped over to the kitchen counter. "I'll take this bowl of soup over to him. I've had more than my fill already."

Jessica gave her a look. "And the chores?" she demanded, frowning.

"After I have it fixed, Mama, I promise."

Jessica stood and stared at her wily daughter. She said nothing however, so Marta took this as tacit consent and stepped to the door. "So Mama, tell me, why did you come back so quickly?" she asked before leaving.

"I forgot my money, young lady, and practically no-one gives you credit on anything these days," replied her mother, huffed.

Marta averted her mother's eyes and noticed that she had averted hers, too.

They both knew the other had lied.

CHAPTER FIVE

"Hi Yosef, are you busy?" Marta asked.

"Marta! Well, not really, why? What is it?"

Yosef glanced at the stool dangling from Marta's right hand and grinned. "What happened to that poor old stool? That's a sturdy one. I remember making it for your father."

Marta grinned. "Well, ahem, Yosef, not sturdy enough, it seems, for it broke."

"How did it break?" Yosef asked, intrigued.

"Well, Uncle Yitzhak, the fattest Cantor that exists in the land, you know him of course, came to visit. I think he sat on it for too long." She laughed.

"Or maybe ate too much while he was on it," Yosef suggested with a smile.

Marta rocked with laughter.

Yosef reached out for the stool. "Here, let me have a look."

She handed it over to him and he placed on his workbench. Marta then gave him the bowl of soup she had cradled in her left arm, and was happy to see him smile. He lifted the lid and sniffed at the food. He gave a sigh of pleasure and took the bowl into the kitchen.

When he came back he examined the stool for damage. His eyes narrowed as he spied a small pebble embedded in the wood. Yosef shrugged his shoulders and pried it loose with a knife he fished out from under his belt.

"Marta, why is this stool wet?"

"Um, it was all dusty and dirty and I thought I'd bring it over washed, or at least, um, rinsed."

"There was no need, for that. After I fix it I'll even wax it for you. Wait here, it won't take long. Yosef took the stool and placed it back on his workbench. "Marta," he then said over his shoulder.

"Yes, Yosef?"

Yosef's voice had sounded deeper than usual, so Marta's reply was quick and eager.

"Do me a favour and please tell your mother to stop giving me so many leftovers. She is making me quite fat!" Yosef gave his short deep belly laugh.

Marta said nothing.

Hearing no response, Yosef turned round and looked at her, turned back to his bench, then turned to look again, this time directly into her beautiful, green, almond-shaped eyes. He noticed that they were flecked with gold. Wavy locks of golden hair seemed to link to each other like gold rings on her pale white forehead, which peeked from under her spotless white shawl. Her face flushed becomingly.

The truth started to dawn on him.

"It's not her is it? It's not your mother sending me all this food practically every day?"

Marta did not reply but hung her head in embarrassment, still managing however to keep her eyes trained searchingly on Yosef's face.

"It is you, isn't it, Marta?"

Marta still said nothing, just got even redder in the face, her eyes now wide and imploring. She lowered her head even further, embarrassed.

"Why?" he asked her; then tried to find an answer to his own question.

"I know I'm a friendly neighbour, and try very hard not to make too much noise when working, especially in the afternoon. And true, I have given your family quite a lot of scrap wood for your stove over the years. But why are you being so kind to me? It is too much, really!"

Marta still did not answer but raised her head slowly to face him directly. Her eyes were glazed, and finally their unspoken reply sank in.

"You like me, don't you? That's it!" he declared, a wide grin developing on his face.

Marta nodded vigorously, her slim body visibly trembling now. Her bony hands were clasped tightly together, her knees knocking.

Yosef stood and stared at the teenage girl. He now noticed that she was dressed too well for a weekday: in that vividly coloured skirt and embroidered white blouse; just for the short hop across the alley to his workshop. Her blond hair looked recently washed even though most of it was tucked under that spotless white veil. Even her shoes, apparently new, shone back at him. Looking up slowly to her face he realised for the first time what a beautiful woman she had become and felt bucked at the thought of what she clearly felt for him.

"And you?" Her words were like a soft patter of rain.

"Me?" he asked.

"Yes, you!" she replied, agitated, aloud.

"Me what?" he asked in irritation.

"You," she repeated, "do you like me too?"

Yosef looked down, then looked past her, and her face fell. She lowered her head and stared at the ground with an expression of shock and disbelief. The ground stared back at her: cold, hard and unfeeling. Then she raised her face to his again, and bit her lower lip to stop it from trembling.

"Marta ...," Yosef started, paused, and then went on, "you are a beautiful young girl. And a pretty good cook too!" He added with a grin. Then a thought struck him, and he jerked a huge thumb at the kitchen doorway.

"Those are not even really leftovers, are they?"

Marta patted her hair, bent her head to one side, and then looked away, confirming his suspicion. She then looked back into his eyes and her pointedly arched eyebrows reminded him he had not yet given her an answer.

"Of course I like you ...! But," Yosef then added hastily, "I don't think I like you in the way you seem to wish ... It would be unkind for me to lead you on," he then concluded flatly.

Marta stood knees together, trembling. Her demeanour betrayed feelings of dismay, shame and anger. She looked like she wanted to run away but couldn't. She averted her eyes, humiliated.

Yosef felt distinctly ill at ease and embarrassed. He realised now just how much she must have fallen in love with him over the past few weeks.

After what seemed like an eternity, Marta gave an abrupt, resolute nod and turned to walk away, only to stop suddenly in her tracks. She twisted on her heels and came back to him.

"Yosef, I know this is all too sudden for you. I don't expect you to want me, to love me outright, that is. People can get to like one another over time, can't they? Love can grow, can it not?" Her tone was pleading now.

The young girl's love for him fairly radiated out of her, and Yosef was once more struck by Marta's remarkable beauty, which seemed emanate from her small face and her slim shapely body like a halo.

He smiled. "Well, yes, of course. I should think it would be very, very hard for *any* man to not love someone as beautiful as you."

Marta's eyes shone, and she gasped her relief.

"But ..." he continued.

"But what?" Marta asked frantically, her eyes narrowing.

Yosef hesitated for a moment, and then decided to change tack.

"But I cannot afford your dowry!"

"My dowry?" Marta gasped, relieved. "What dowry? We are not wealthy; my father would not expect much."

"Well, he would certainly expect more than I could give him," he asserted.

"No, not at all," she assured him hurriedly. "Besides, he can wait, if anything. You're a hard worker."

"Marta, really." Yosef then decided to come out with the whole truth. "It's not *only* the dowry. I ..." He could not bring himself to say it.

"You have your eyes set on somebody else!" Marta prompted icily.

Yosef's silence gave her the answer she seemed to fear most.

"Who is it?" I demand to know!"

Yosef still remained obstinately silent.

"Don't worry, I think I know who it is," Marta gritted out the words. "That *Maryam*, isn't it?" she yelled.

Yosef was impressed by her perspicuity, and he nodded.

"Why? Why *her*? She is not even half as beautiful as me," Marta whined, "and she cannot cook, cannot sew!" Marta started to blurt out all the inside information on her friend that came to her mind. "Her father is also strict, very strict. He will boss you around! And she is as tall as a man!"

"Yet ...," Yosef said gently.

Marta's eyes glistened. "Yet you still want *her*, don't you? Even though you know perfectly well that all I've just said about her is true." She said in anger.

"Yes, but if it were not for her, seriously, I don't think I'd have eyes for anyone other than you."

Marta glared. Through her teeth she continued, "And, furthermore, for your information, on her part, well, she likes someone else. She's in love with Shimon. She adores him, in fact. He's like her, witty; very witty. He is even going to become a Pharisee one day. Her father will love that! They'd make a perfect couple. Do you think she'd be happy just with—?" She stopped in mid-sentence.

Yosef finished it for her, "... with just a dumb, lumbering carpenter?"

"Yes!" Marta confirmed defiantly.

"But *you* would?

"*Yes I would!*" She stressed each word angrily. "As for Maryam, she's too clever. She continually needs mental stimulation. Why, she even reads scrolls, just like a man! They have some at her house. I've seen them. They're her father's. She will get bored with you, in due course, whereas I never will!"

"Maybe," Yosef said, in a pensive tone. "Well, as for her liking Shimon, I suppose she will simply have to choose." He paused for a moment. "Unless her father chooses for her, of course."

"Yes, but in *my* case I do not have to choose," Marta said pleadingly. "I cannot choose."

She thought for a moment then declared sagely, "if love were a choice, I don't think it would be real love at all."

Yosef stiffened at this. Encouraged she caught his eyes.

"Yosef, it is you that I want, and only you. And I swear by the living God, I will make you happy."

"But I cannot help it, either." Yosef almost yelled at her. "Don't you see? There is something about her that I want that I cannot explain. Maybe it's as you say, love cannot be a choice."

"I'll tell you what you cannot explain," Marta replied sarcastically, "what you cannot explain is how you are not worried about affording *her* dowry, yet worried about mine! When everybody knows her family is wealthier than mine, and so her father would expect more."

Yosef felt ashamed at being caught out.

"Yes Marta, I'm sorry to have said that earlier. I just did not want to hurt your feelings further, that's all. And, I do mean to speak to Yehoyaqim about the dowry and all."

Marta gritted her teeth, and hissed through them, eyes narrowing again to slits, "Yes, you speak to him. I wish you luck!"

Upon which she turned swiftly on her heels, rushed out and fled back to her house.

Just as he heard the slam of the door, he realised he still had the stool in his hand.

"Wait!" he called after her. He opened the door, stood on the doorstep and looked over at Marta's house across the alley, his face crestfallen. His eyes wandered to the side and fell on Ribqah, who was squatting like a crow in the shady corner of the alley. A cat slept on her lap. She grinned back through her gums at him. He scowled at her, stepped back inside and slammed the door shut.

CHAPTER SIX

At the village well, Maryam heaved the two heavy wooden buckets of water up off the wide stone rim with a grunt, and then started up the hill towards her house.

"Here, Maryam. I'll carry those for you!"

There was no mistaking Yosef's booming voice. He put down his own two enormous buckets and held out his paw-like hands towards her.

"Why, thank you, Yosef," Maryam replied graciously, "but I'm a big strong girl, you know. I can carry them easily enough."

"I'm sure you can, Maryam." Yosef smiled.

Ignoring her feeble protestations, he took hold of her buckets and walked by her side back up the hill.

"So, tell me," Maryam asked, "are you making anything interesting at the moment?"

"Well, not really, just the odd stool, and doors, and things," he replied. "But, I do have a lot of repair work, too."

"They say you never stop?" She asked, beaming at him.

"Yes, true, I do not stop really, except for a bite or two, of delicious food though ..."

Maryam noticed him suddenly turning red after he said this. *Was that a look of guilt?* She wondered whatever could have caused it.

Then he went on, "I don't get tired easily, thank God, and I really cannot afford to stop, in any case, you see. So when there is nothing else to do, I simply saw planks out of logs."

"Don't you get bored, Yosef?" Maryam asked him. "I mean, one plank looks like any other." She chuckled and arranged her long silky black hair, which was could never be completely covered by her veil.

"I do at times, for in my line of work there is no one to talk to. But I love everything about wood—the smell, the texture—and that keeps me happy. I love creating things out of raw material. Wood is something that is real, that is still alive, in some way, I believe. And if taken care of, it lasts for centuries. It is softer than iron, yet strangely, can outlive it."

Maryam laughed. "I'm surprised at hearing such deep philosophical thoughts coming from you, Yosef! Why, you sound like a proper rabbi!"

"So I'm not the big dolt everyone thinks I am, eh?" he asked, grinning back at her.

She then sensed that he had noticed she was slowing her pace, and secretly hoped he'd think it was so as not to rush him with his heavy load. They then stopped to allow a heavily laden cart to rumble past.

"No, not everyone, Yosef, I'm sure." She fluttered her eyes at him. "On the contrary, in my case, I think of you as a gentle giant. And everybody also says you are a just man, and very kind-hearted." Maryam's eyes glowed. She continued, "Now that is what I like most about you. Because any another man, given your size, might easily fall into the temptation of being arrogant and a bully. You, on the contrary, do not. Why, you even take the back seat at the synagogue. I've noticed that. You have the heart of a saint."

"Has word got out then?"

"What? About what?"

"About the Leper's Community at Gadara, I mean."

Maryam stopped in her tracks at the mention of the dreaded Lepers' Community that was situated several miles east of Nazaret, by the hills of Gadara.

The place was given a wide berth by everyone. It had grown steadily over the years as many who contracted leprosy from all over the surrounding area came to settle there. The Lepers scraped out a living painstakingly tilling the extremely hard, pebbly soil on the hills, and using what meagre grazing ground the surrounding area could offer. They tried to lead normal lives as much as they could, with some couples even raising children.

"What about it, Yosef?" Maryam asked, her voice hardening.

Yosef said nothing. A cold chill rose up her spine. She shivered, then feebly asked, "So then it is true isn't it ... what they say ...?"

"Yes, Maryam, I *have* done some work for them. I admit to it."

Maryam shuddered, clasped her hands together and took a step back.

He lowered the buckets to the ground, and sighing, turned to face her.

"Why? Whatever for? Are you crazy?" she yelled over at him, hands on her hips.

"Maybe, maybe I am at that." Yosef replied sadly. "But, they had two ploughs broken recently, nothing to till the land with, you see? They would all have starved eventually, had I not—"

"But ...," Maryam started.

"Don't you worry Maryam. It's alright. Really. You see, they had sent their request to me through Azaryahu as usual ..."

Azaryahu was the only authorised go-between between the Lepers and the villagers. He was robust and healthy and was obliged to call on the physician upon arrival before approaching anyone. Although his health was thus ironically monitored more than anyone else's, he was still nevertheless given a wide berth by all and sundry.

"And I arranged to meet them halfway," Yosef explained. "They did not bring the ploughs into our village of course, nor did I enter their settlement. They left them for me at the roadside and I carried my tools over, and whatever wood and other materials necessary. Could not risk using the donkey, though. Everything went on my back. I mended them right there in a clearing beside the road.

"Hard work in the sun, I ended up exhausted, I can tell you," he concluded with a wan smile.

"You're mad!" Maryam repeated flatly, but she could not bring herself to shout at him anymore.

"Maybe," he said, "but I took all the precautions, of course. Whitewashed the damn ploughs in slaked lime before I even touched them. I also whitewashed my tools afterwards. Heck, I even whitewashed myself." He laughed. "I looked like a corpse as I dried in the scorching sun. Couldn't wait to rinse the damn stuff off!"

He straightened up and beamed, then pointed two index fingers at his face. "See, I'm fine, and somewhat pale-skinned, like some scribe."

They both laughed.

"Does anyone else know?" Maryam asked, stepping closer to him and resuming her walk.

"I don't think so, except for old Ribqah maybe."

"That old hag!" exclaimed Maryam.

"I don't think I'd quite rinsed all the lime-wash off properly before I went back home, you see." He laughed. "And her eyes are like those of a hawk."

"More like those of a crow," Maryam said indignantly. "You are mad, Yosef," she told him once again, but this time with a hint of endearment in her voice. "Are you sure it wasn't for the money? Are you maybe doing badly, Yosef? Go on, tell me!"

"What money? They *have* no money, Maryam. They promised me payment come harvest time. I doubt I shall ever get it. Their fields are in a patch of impossibly hard ground, dry and windswept too, that no-one else would bother with."

"You should not have taken the risk, Yosef. Only the very old can afford to deal with Lepers. They have nothing to lose, and their only gain is in God's esteem for their kindness.

"And don't do it again!" her voice was loud and angry. "If you contract the disease you'll be drummed straight out of the village. Your selfless motives will not make the least bit of difference to anyone."

"I'll try, Maryam, I promise you that, but if I didn't fix their things no-one else would have."

"Well, there's Shimon?" she ventured.

"Shimon?" Yosef gave a laugh. "Not likely."

"Is it because he has lots of orders?"

"No." Yosef grinned. "Shimon never refuses work, however much he has already. Why do you think I'm not doing so well? He takes the bulk of it, practically mops it all up. But there's no way he'd do any work for the Lepers."

Shaking his huge head, he, continued in a cynical tone, "They might die before they paid him, you see."

After a pause he asked her, "You like him, that Shimon, Maryam, don't you?"

Maryam felt waves of embarrassment and irritation. Stopping, she turned to face him.

"Yes I do," she replied defiantly.

Yosef's face turned grim.

She hurried to explain, "he makes me laugh, Yosef. He is brilliant, as you must know. And I like that."

"But ... he is just a friend," she clarified hastily.

Yosef gave a grunt and started walking again.

She ran after him and asked, impishly, "but tell me, how do you know that I like him?"

Yosef was about to mention Marta, but decided to answer differently, if still as truthfully.

"He told me so. He came over to my workshop to choose some planks a few days ago. I was surprised, I hadn't seen him for quite a while."

Maryam nodded, and he went on, "we were talking, and he said he plans to ask for your hand." His voice fell as he said this.

"Well, he can ask for it until the coming of the Messiah. I'll not have him!" she hissed.

Yosef could not hide his pleasure at this. He put down his buckets and wagged a heavy finger at her, "it's not actually your choice, surely you must know that!"

"Maybe not," she replied, stomping her foot down hard. "But should he want to proceed with his plans despite my wishes, he will have one hell of a shrew for a wife from the very day of our wedding!"

They both laughed at this, and Maryam slapped Yosef's shoulder. Then she moved as close to him as the bucket he was carrying could allow.

They walked on till they spied a couple of women coming down the hill, carrying buckets, and they discreetly stepped away from each other. After the couple had passed on, they drew closer again and continued up the gently sloping hill until Maryam came to a sudden halt. Yosef stopped too and looked at her, raising his eyebrows.

"So, Yosef?" she asked, very softly. She looked directly into his eyes, and he looked straight back into hers. Everything around them seemed to fade. Yosef did not even put down the heavy buckets; their weight seemed to have dissolved.

"So ...?" she asked again.

"So?" he echoed.

"So, do you want me to be your wife?" And then she added with a laugh, "I can't wait forever, you know, for you to ask."

"You *know* I do, Maryam, you wouldn't have dared to be the first to ask otherwise."

Maryam acknowledged his outspokenness by nodding impishly. She trembled in excitement, and gasped, "Then you'd better not waste any more time!"

She resolved to make him aware of the manoeuvrings in the game of love that women knew instinctively, whereas most men seemed to have to be taught.

"You should not have let Shimon try to dissuade you. *That's* why he came over to your place to tell you about his plans. For God's sake, don't let him be the first one to ask my father for my hand! He might take him at his word, heavens forbid!"

Maryam was frantic.

"I won't, Maryam, I promise you. I'll come over and see your father."

"But before you promise me that, you have to promise me one more thing."

"What?"

"That you do not expose yourself to the Lepers ever again."

"I've already promised you!" he retorted.

"No, you promised you'd *try* not to. You must promise you *won't*!"

Yosef hesitated, then nodded.

"Alright, I promise you, I won't. After all, those two ploughs I fixed for them should last them a lifetime." He chuckled.

They had come to the alley at the end of which Maryam's house stood, noticeably higher than those around it.

Maryam put her hands on Yosef's as they gripped the buckets, and left them there for a while, before sliding them to the bucket handles. She gave a heave. But Yosef did not let go. He looked again deep into her eyes and then he shuddered as though a sudden thought had struck him. He shook it off and then abruptly let go of the buckets, grinning as she grimaced at their weight.

"When will you be back at the well?" He asked gently.

"The day after tomorrow, around the same time."

"Good, I will see you there." Yosef nodded, turned and, his head hung low, made his way pensively, back downhill towards the well. Maryam trudged her way to her house, straining at the weight—and thinking deeply about his abrupt change of mood.

****

Yosef too wondered at that strange chill he had unexpectedly felt. *He should be the happiest man in the world. The girl he loves, loves him back. She even proposed to him! Unheard of! He shook his head and took a deep breath. I am going to have the family I've always dreamed of, he assured himself: a life simple and beautiful, like wood; at one with nature, at peace with God. That was the sum total of all he ever wanted in life. So why this sudden bout of doubt, of sadness even? Wet feet? Impossible!*

He shrugged it off. *Maybe it was true. He must be working too much.*

YOSEF AND MARYAM

CHAPTER SEVEN

"You're overloading that ass, Shimon," remarked Nethanel.

Nethanel was the old factotum at the jetty at Tverya, a little village on the south shore of the sea of Hagalil. And his eye was an experienced one, including in matters not solely related to the sea.

Onto the back of an ass which stood tethered to a twisted and weathered pole, Shimon had been loading all kinds of furniture items from a huge pile which had been unceremoniously dumped onto the jetty off a boat earlier on that morning.

The shipment consisted of the entire contents of the house of a debtor of Shimon's: one who had the gall of dying suddenly, and worse still, dying insolvent. Shimon had laid claim to, and won, his entire earthly belongings: which were not much, since he had been destitute, and had lived in a tiny hovel.

But the carpenter was relieved to see that it could just about cover the debt, perhaps even exceed it somewhat.

And he was not about to leave anything of any value behind, especially to that sea-washed gaggle of fishermen at Tverya.

So he ignored Nethanel's unsolicited advice. The beleaguered ass was veering comically from side to side according to the weight and location of each additional object being loaded. Although Shimon was trying desperately to balance the load, the beast was panting and clearly under a great deal of strain.

An old salt tramped over.

"Hey, you! You are over loading that ass!" he barked.

Shimon gave him a scowl.

In defiance he heaved a teak commode right onto the middle of the poor ass's back. The ass whinnied, and whined. Shimon quickly secured the item with a length of hemp rope before it could slide off.

A group of people started gathering around, amused at the spectacle. Shimon began to get more and more irritated.

"Why are you overloading that ass?"

The rasping voice came from behind Shimon's shoulder and he spun, a nasty retort ready on his lips. It never left them, however. For the comment came from a white haired, white bearded, old priest who, short and bent like a hook at the shoulders, was wagging a bony finger up at him

Instead, Shimon benefited the venerable old gentleman with a polite answer. "Rabbi, I have no one to help me here, you see. I have to take all this furniture away at one go. So with all due respect, I really have no choice. If I leave something behind to fetch it later, who do I have to watch over it? I know no one here. Don't worry about the ass. It can take the load; it is not more than six years old, and very strong."

The old priest looked at him quizzically.

"I also plan to give it a rest it on the way," Shimon added graciously. "Think I would trust my property on the jetty with this lot around? He waved his arm in a circle around him and wrinkled his nose at his detractors. The priest shook his head. Shimon was not sure whether it was in reprimand or agreement, so he continued loading the furniture.

"Hey, you're overloading that poor ass," a deep voice boomed behind him.

Shimon spun round in fury to look up at a towering figure. *Yosef of all people!*

"You too, Yosef? Hey, it's my ass! My ass! Get it? I can overload it as much as I want to! D'you hear?" He swept his arm in a circle and jabbed an angry finger at the crowd. Don't you lot have anything else to do but to whine and give *unsolicited* advice? Have you nothing else to do, I say! Is it already the Sabbath for you, or what? Or maybe you expect to get paid for your advice? If you're so sorry for this ass why don't you come to its aid by relieving it of some of its burden? By carrying some of the stuff for me? All the way up to Nazaret?

"Eh, Yosef, what do *you* say? You're certainly big enough for it! And given that you seem to have absolutely no work to do, it might even earn you a denarius!"

Yosef was visibly offended. The onlookers waited for his reaction, but whatever they expected did not materialise, for Yosef simply gritted his teeth and scowled at Shimon.

Shimon sneered and surveyed the rest of the stuff on the jetty. The advice he had been given did have some effect on him, however, for he now realised he simply could not load *everything* on the struggling ass's back. So he started making quick mental calculations, offsetting in his mind the weight versus the value of the items that remained: a pair of stools, a small box of rusty tools, a dusty carpet, and other more expensive items. *Could he actually take a chance and leave some of it behind? After all, the priest had witnessed the situation, and that by itself would perhaps dissuade any pilferage.*

His eyes fell on a beautiful wooden menorah. *'I'm not going to leave that behind for sure,'* he thought. He heaved it up. It had a high stand, was made of solid oak, and it was heavy. He placed it on the ass's back and the animal let out a gasp. His spectators glared at him. Ignoring them he deftly strapped the item in place, then turned round and sneered at them. After ostensibly noting down a list of the items left on the jetty, he gathered everything in a pile and covered them with the dusty old carpet.

Shimon then started to lead the heavily panting ass off. It managed two steps, and then halted. It would not move. Shimon yanked again at the reins. Still the ass would not budge. The group on the jetty started to snigger, but Shimon's ferocious glare dissuaded any further comment.

He yanked again and the ass collapsed all at once, legs akimbo on the ground. It screamed out in pain. Shimon panicked, fell to his knees beside it, and frantically started unstrapping the load. The ass drummed its rear legs, gasped for each ragged breath, and started foaming at the mouth and nostrils. Although Shimon looked around pleadingly, no one offered to help untie the load. The onlookers scowled and sneered back at him in disgust. The ass's eyes dimmed and its big eyelids drooped. Shimon was sure its heart would give out. In his panic he was making little progress with untying the straps.

Suddenly, the ass was heaved onto its feet and over his head, by some miraculous force. Shimon looked up to see Yosef straining at the load.

"What are you looking at, Shimon?!" gasped Yosef between his teeth. The veins in his red neck seemed about to burst.

"Come on, untie the load, quickly, you fool!"

Yosef was heaving the load upwards, taking the weight off the ass which, with a couple of kicks, rose to its legs, all four of which were shaking and looking still most unsteady. The two men were then surrounded by the onlookers, some of whom proceeded to help Yosef support the load while others undid the straps and yanked off the topmost items.

Yosef raised a hand to stop them when he calculated a load that the ass could take, even given its state.

Shimon's face felt in flames. He stared at the ground, and without a word, meekly let Yosef take charge of the situation.

"Know what, Shimon?"

Yosef was panting and still had more than a touch of anger in his voice, "since, as you say, I have no work today, I can stay here for you until dusk, and watch over the pile. You need to make two trips to take everything."

Shimon realised he had no choice but to agree, and this made him angry.

"For a whole denarius, mind you!" Yosef's voice was ragged, and brooked no haggling.

Shimon nodded reluctantly. Barely audible, he ventured, "Will you help me load it as well?"

Yosef sneered, but nodded his assent all the same.

"And on the last trip I will help you offload it too," he assured him icily.

With a sigh, Yosef leaned back to rest onto the log railing of the jetty, while Shimon, his head hung low, led the still faltering ass off towards the road to Nazaret. As he felt everyone's eyes on his back, he stumbled and swore under his breath, hardly able to choke back his fury.

CHAPTER EIGHT

"Yehoyaqim!" The call was barely above a whisper, and Yehoyaqim did not hear it.

He was, as was his wont, on his knees in the centre of the Synagogue, deeply lost in prayer. The sexton, who saw him every single day, had so gotten used to him that he practically considered him part of the furniture. He never greeted him; did not expect any greeting in return. And it was not the first time that he jumped whenever Yehoyaqim made some sudden movement, so rigid and immobile was he, each and every afternoon. Even his devout prayers were but a droning murmur and unintelligible to any but himself. No one had ever dared disturb him. Until now.

"Yehoyaqim!" This time the call was louder. Yehoyaqim twitched. But if he heard, he heeded not.

After the lapse of a minute or two his name was finally yelled out.

"Yehoyaqim!" And this time the elderly gentleman's head lifted up and turned round, an angry retort at the ready.

But this was never uttered, for it was the priest himself, Hananiah, who he saw was calling him.

"What is it Rev Hananiah?" Yehoyaqim asked, not without a touch of steel in his deep voice.

"I beg your pardon, Yehoyaqim, but I must ask you to move."

"Move?" Yehoyaqim could not believe what he was hearing.

"Yes, it is necessary."

"Necessary?"

Yehoyaqim's capacity to speak seemed limited to echoing the priest.

"Yes, I'm afraid we are bound to finish it before the Sabbath."

"Bound?"

This was starting to sound ridiculous, and now it was the priest's turn to heat up.

"Yes, Yehoyaqim," he replied coldly. "Would I ask you to move unless we were bound?"

"Bound by whom?"

The priest stared at him.

"By Shimon, of course!" he replied.

"Shimon? Which Shimon?"

"The carpenter!"

"So," Yehoyaqim exclaimed sarcastically, "pray tell me now, how can you or I, or any elder of this Synagogue, be bound by a Carpenter?"

"Have you not heard?"

"Heard what?"

"We are finally replacing the altar railing."

It was now Yehoyaqim's turn to gaze at the priest.

Of course he was fully aware that the small but ancient railing needed replacing, for it had been missing for over two weeks now.

He remembered hearing it shatter to pieces himself.

Old Yitzhak, the Cantor, had had a fatal heart attack one evening and, grabbing at it in his final moments, had brought it down with him, as he rolled and sprawled on the shattering wood. It was as if he had reached out to God to spare him: to no avail.

Both Yitzhak and the railing had met their end together. It was also quite unfortunate, or more likely the work of the Devil, that the Cantor, who was also the village butcher, happened to be the fattest and heaviest member of the Community. Furthermore, in the trampling rush to come to his aid, as well as in their attempts to raise it back, the congregation had further damaged the railing beyond any hope of repair.

But Yehoyaqim had not heard that it was finally being replaced, until now. He softened visibly.

"So why now?" he asked.

"Why not now?

"Why not in the morning? Some other day, in the morning?"

"Shimon has just finished the railing, and he has brought it over, loaded on his ass. It's outside by the gate. He wants the job completed before sundown. Insists on it."

"Insists?"

Yehoyaqim seemed about to revert to his previous manner of speech. But the priest would not have it.

"Insists! Yes, insists!" he yelled.

"So now the Carpenter, whom we hire, insists!" Yehoyaqim yelled back icily.

"We did not hire him!" the priest shouted.

Yehoyaqim stared blankly at him.

The priest did not wait for yet another parroted reply. He quickly explained, "The carpenter made it, and is donating it to us for free."

"For free?"

"Yes, for free, and including the installation!" The priest smiled, happy at being the one to break the good news to the venerable Yehoyaqim.

Finally Yehoyaqim stood up, feeling pleased, very pleased.

Of course, the craftsman could make his own conditions if he was donating his work for free.

"That is excellent" he said, clapping his hands together. "Go on, go on! Tell him he can start right now." With a flick of his fingers, he shooed the priest out of the Synagogue to summon Shimon.

"See," he shouted after him in glee, "Rev Hananiah, all is not yet lost with the young generation!"

But either Shimon had the gift of intuition, or he had been eavesdropping on them, for his beaming face promptly appeared at the doorway. He strode valiantly in, and shook hands first with the priest and then with Yehoyaqim. The latter pumped his hand, thanking him volubly and bestowing on him a multitude of blessings. Shimon's grin stretched from ear to ear. Then he gingerly pulled his hand away.

"Rev Yehoyaqim, excuse me, but we really must start on it now, right away, for it would be a disaster should the Sabbath come upon us before we are ready."

Yehoyaqim nodded his head vigorously, and made for the door so as to let him work in peace.

He then stopped, spun round and asked, "Do you need my assistance, young man? Although, you must know, I'm not young any more, of course ..."

"No, not at all," replied Shimon, "but thank you, anyway. By this evening, you will find it ready."

Yehoyaqim grinned and sailed through the door, his heart singing along with his lips as he made his way home.

CHAPTER NINE

Yosef was bored waiting for Shimon. There was nothing to do in the harbour at Tverya except watch the odd seagull swinging and circling in the sky above. He had been waiting for over three hours and Shimon should really have been back by now.

The sun had risen high overhead, the heat was fierce and what little breeze blew over from the sea of Hagalil gave only limited relief. He had long since crossed over to the other side of the dusty harbour road, where he had found some shade under the tattered awning of an old boarded-up fishing shack, which was built out of the most irregular blocks of stone Yosef had ever seen in his life.

With his back propped up against its rough wall he looked over Shimon's dusty mound at the sole fishing boat that remained drawn ashore, unlike all the other boats, which had long been out at sea.

In the shade that it gave a young lad had set about cleaning a net from the dried debris that was entangled in it.

The scene flashed him back to the time when he often used to do the same work as a child; an entire day's work for just one miserable denarius.

He would leave Nazaret for Tverya before dawn and he would work non-stop until dark.

And although he had done the task many times his mind wandered to that one time he would never forget, for as long as he lived ...

"Yosef!"

Yosef did not look up. The boy was sitting in a corner, engrossed in cleaning out a huge net from strands of seaweed, crabs and other dry debris.

He was making good progress and in an hour or two would finish the job and claim the denarius promised to him by the old fisherman. Although barely twelve, Yosef was already as big as many of the men around him. The harbour was crowded, and a veritable hub of activity; and his friend Abner, who was calling him, had had a hard time in finding him.

"Yosef, here you are!" Abner shouted, rushing over to his friend as he finally spotted him. He was breathless. "Are you deaf or what? I couldn't see you. I called out for you God knows how many times."

"What is it Abner," asked Yosef, disinterestedly, not even looking up from his work.

"Stop whatever you're doing and come with me, quickly! Back towards Nazaret ... we do not have much time, maybe they've started already!" His friend replied excitedly.

"Started what?" Yosef muttered.

"You haven't heard?" Abner asked incredulously.

"Heard what? What's going on? A funeral? Wedding? Whose?"

Abner smiled cynically. Perhaps he remembered that Yosef had been sleeping over at Tverya ever since the Sabbath, for *over two days now, so he could be excused for not knowing.*

An impish grin appeared on Abner's face.

"Come on, leave everything, you'll see!" He grabbed his friend by the arm.

Yosef resisted, and shook his arm clear, "wait, Abner, you have to tell me why first! What is it? I can't just leave the work half-finished! I won't be paid!"

"Oh come on, Yosef! The pay doesn't matter, you don't want to miss this; it's worth it! You can do the work some other time!"

Yosef stood up, his curiosity piqued.

"What is it, though? Tell me and then *I'll decide whether it's worth leaving for or not!"*

"No I won't," teased Abner. "You just have to take my word for it."

"Well, I'm not coming then," replied Yosef flatly, and promptly sat down again on his low stool.

"Yosef, I do not want to tell you simply so as to have it come as a surprise to you. That will make it much more fun! Get it? Trust me, will you? Come on!" The boy's face shone with such eagerness and excitement that Yosef, intrigued, scrambled up again.

"Alright, alright, I'll come with you, back to Nazaret. Mind you," he then added, glaring down at his grinning friend. "If it turns out not to be worth it you will have to pay me the half denarius I'm going to lose because of this."

Abner's grin faded; but still resolute, he nodded.

"Agreed!" he shouted, "so now, get a move on!"

Yosef strode over to the old fisherman who was deftly coiling a clean net onto the aft deck of his boat.

"Yona, listen, something has come up. I have to go back to Nazaret right away, I'm sorry."

The old salt glanced over Yosef's net, which lay in two heaps: unfinished.

"But you haven't finished it yet!"

"Yes I know that, I'm sorry. I really have to go now. It's more than three-quarters finished, but I'll settle for half the money. Just half a denarius will do!"

Yona glared at Yosef, and scowled at Abner, who was still tugging his friend away.

"Half-finished, three quarters, makes no difference. Yosef, you either finish the whole job or you get nothing! It's no use to me half-finished!"

Yosef's eyes flared with anger. "Then I want nothing, you finish it yourself," he shouted back at the fisherman. "You can keep your miserable half denarius!" He tramped off in disgust, with Abner following swiftly.

"Damn miser!" Yosef muttered under his breath. He turned to Abner. "See I lost a whole denarius! This had better be good Abner!" he warned.

"It will be, Yosef, trust me." Abner grinned as they tramped steadily up the hill towards Nazaret.

YOSEF AND MARYAM

CHAPTER TEN

"I do not pay you to sleep!"

Startled by the shrill voice, Yosef opened his eyes to behold Shimon, hot and dishevelled, astride his ass, glaring down at him.

Yosef was sitting with his back to the wall of an old fisherman's shack.

"I wasn't asleep!" he protested. "You took ages, I was just remembering ..."

Shimon did not let him finish.

"Well, asleep or not, your eyes were closed; I saw them; and I am the one who stands to lose here, if something gets stolen! *Watching* over my property indeed!"

Shimon scowled.

"I have sharp ears, Shimon," replied Yosef, with a smile, getting up and deciding to make a joke out of it.

Shimon hopped off the ass, and fished out the scroll where he had listed the items he had left behind.

"There's no need for that," Yosef assured him. No-one would dare touch anything."

Shimon sized the big man up and down. He grunted and stuffed the tiny scroll back into his leather purse.

"Come on, let's load it up!"

They soon loaded the ass up with the remaining items.

Shimon even decided to leave a rickety old stool behind which he assessed as good for nothing except to weigh the ass down unnecessarily.

They made their way up the rough, yet gently sloping road to Nazaret, and within an hour or so were within sight of the village. The ass was panting heavily by now. Shimon decided to skirt the steep hill that lay directly in their path and take a secondary, less arduous, route. One that was indeed longer but much less demanding. They passed around a dark and despondent stony outcrop into a rock-strewn clearing, stopped and looked around.

"There's no chance of my taking *this* route at night," Shimon said, moving quickly on again, and tugging the ass after him.

Yosef remained where he was. His eyes narrowed as he spotted something on the ground. Walking over, he tugged at a piece of black cloth that had been bleached grey by the sun, as it lay caught between two stones. He smoothed it out on the ground and was not surprised to see that it had broken threads of silvery embroidery still on it. He froze, closed his eyes, and the scene from the past came back to him in a rush ...

"Hey, what are we taking this route for?" Yosef asked Abner who had opted to skirt the last hill to Nazaret, and take the longer route instead.

"Save your breath for walking," Abner panted.

They turned around a huge rock and a hubbub of voices, including much yelling and screaming, could be heard. Abner smiled and Yosef quickened his step. They came to the other side of the rock and the scene finally came into full view. Yosef gasped.

A bruised and bloodied woman was standing bare-breasted, half in shadow, in a clearing under a sharp overhang of rock. She was sobbing.

Her tattered blouse, black and embroidered with silver, hung and flailed around her waist in strips as she desperately tried to side-step a barrage of rocks that a huge crowd of people, standing at some distance, were assiduously pelting her with.

"Harlot!" screamed an old man as he hurled a sizeable rock, which however fell short of its target.

Two more rocks came flying. She ducked and they passed overhead.

"Whore! Adulteress! Sinner!"

A rock whizzed out of nowhere and hit her squarely on her left breast. A spray of crimson appeared as the woman screamed out in pain. *Yosef stared; he had never seen a bare breasted woman before, except for the odd glimpse of some nursing mother at her doorway. And he was not exactly pleased that this should be how he should see one for the first time.*

"Jezebel!" someone screamed.

The mob was composed of men and women of all ages. Old Ribqah was at the forefront, her hands on her hips and a satisfied look in her sunken, bloodshot eyes. Children were also present. Some of the younger ones were weeping; terrified at the scene, and hiding behind their mother's skirts, from where they took a peek from time to time. None of the mothers were throwing stones. *Boys of about his age were the most enthusiastic about stoning the woman however, and quite a few of them were jeering and laughing as they took aim and let fly at her. Shimon was up front at the head of the group, but his aim was terrible. He missed, and missed yet again, and the others were poking fun at him.*

"Hey Shimon, why don't you go right up to her!" one said. "You're bound to get her for sure then!"

"And someone would get you *for sure, too," said another, who laughed hysterically as he took aim and threw.*

Shimon looked up at the hail of stones and rocks arching overhead and wisely decided to maintain a safe distance from the target.

Abner rushed down to be greeted by his friends and, scooping up an armful of rocks, as if to make up for lost time, quickly started launching them in rapid succession, hardly bothering to aim.

Yosef walked down, paused for a moment, then picking up a rock, he threw it and missed. He threw another and missed again, this time to the other side. The others laughed at him, and he grimaced.

A loud scream, and then a moan rose from the woman, as a rock landed on her mouth and sent most of her front teeth flying. Sputtering blood, she sagged to her knees. After a while she looked up. One of her eyes had been reduced to a large and blackish lump. With her other eye, she looked fixedly at Yosef.

Yosef froze. He felt that strange eye imploring him to do something, an eye that was coloured a beautiful emerald green. It was untouched, and glistened like some jewel under its thin arched black eyebrow. He understood her plea, and shuddered heavily.

Giving a quick look round, he took a few steps forward and squatted down beside a rock the size of a small barrel. Yosef grunted as he heaved it close to his chest, and wrapping his arms around it, staggered as he strode heavily with it towards the victim. Rocks had continued flying from all directions; he was struck on his back a couple of times as he drew closer to the target. He halted, wincing at the pain, then gritting his teeth, continued determinedly on his way towards the woman.

"Watch out Yosef, you crazy fool!" Abner yelled, alarmed.

Another boy shouted over in glee, "hey Yosef, mind you don't drop that damn mountain on your feet!"

Yosef finally came to a halt at an arm's length from her. Grunting, he raised the rock above his head, and he felt his shuddering biceps bulging almost to the point of splitting. She looked up at the rock, expressionless. Yosef then hurled it down, hitting her squarely on top of her head and driving her to the ground with a dull thud.

The rock was so huge and heavy; it did not even roll over away from the woman's shattered skull. From under it, a crimson flow trailed out, resembling crazily braided hair.

A huge hush fell.

Had Yosef expected some reprimand from the older men and women for his unprecedented action, this never materialised.

Shimon's shrill, jeering yell was the only thing that broke the silence.

"Hey, Yosef, we all know how big and strong you are. You do not have to keep reminding us, I'll have you know!"

His arms held out wide for approval, Shimon turned to look at the others, but no one said anything: the hush remained unbroken.

Yosef ignored him.

He stared at the corpse, for the woman was undoubtedly dead. A flow of yellowish fluid had started tracking its way through the dust as if to meet up with one of the thin, serpent-like rivulets of blood. It hesitated, though, at the last moment, stopped briefly, and then changed direction to trickle on the other way.

Sharp gusts of wind tugged at the tattered dress of the adulteress, exposing her shapely but scratched and bruised thighs. It suddenly seemed to have turned much colder.

One by one, everybody had silently started to leave.

Abner tugged at Yosef's sleeve, who he shook him off, lost in his thoughts.

After a while, Yosef finally turned round and discovered that he was entirely alone. The place was deserted. He was alone in the middle of nowhere with a dead woman. A woman he had just killed: killed with impunity. He blinked rapidly at the realization of what he had just done: and to think he was not yet even a grown-up. What might he do in the future? What has it got in store for him?

He looked up and saw a couple of vultures circling high overhead, in the darkening sky, waiting for him to leave. He crouched down beside the corpse and decided to wait for the gravediggers instead.

It was a long wait, and it was almost completely dark when two bedraggled men finally made their appearance, their lanterns dangling. They muttered and complained as they heaved the rock aside to free up the body, completely ignoring the boy standing by. Yosef stepped back and left them to their work ...

"Yosef, sleeping again?" Shimon's tone was not so hard this time, however. He realised what Yosef was remembering, and did not look at all surprised when the big man tugged the silvery rag free and, scraping a hole in the ground with a jagged piece of rock, proceeded to bury it.

YOSEF AND MARYAM

CHAPTER ELEVEN

Shimon arrived at Yehoyaqim's house and knocked on the door. Hannah answered his soft knock. He had dressed up impeccably in black for the occasion. Ramrod straight, he blinked at her. A hot flush crept up his cheeks.

"Why, Shimon," she said, "what brings you to our house?"

"My greetings, Hannah. I ... I came to see ..."

"Yehoyaqim?" she prompted, smiling, as she thought, *'who else?'*

"Yes," he affirmed, "is he in, by any chance ...?"

Hannah hesitated for a moment, and looked at him out of the corner of her eyes.

Perhaps she'd sensed he already knew very well he was in.

Shimon urged himself to tread more carefully here.

"Yes, in fact he has just come back from prayers," Hannah then replied, "one moment, I'll call him."

As custom would have it, she did not let the young man in, but gently closed the door.

It was soon re-opened by Yehoyaqim.

"Why, Shimon! What brings you to our humble home, young man? Step right in!"

Shimon was aware Yehoyaqim had quite a high opinion of him—he was after all an eager, religious, and generous member of their community.

An opinion that he had lately done his utmost to raise even higher.

He stepped in gingerly, surveying the room discreetly, so as to make a mental note of some lacking item of furniture he could offer them, in time, of course.

With a nervous cough, he started, "Rev Yehoyaqim, I am not that young, as you address me, any more."

Shimon gave a wan smile as he took the seat offered to him by the elderly gentleman.

Yehoyaqim also smiled, raised his eyebrows and waited for a proper answer to his question. Shimon felt extremely agitated, a cold sweat forming on his brow. *And he knew it must show.*

"And," Shimon continued, "since I'm not so young any more, it is now the time to finally find me a suitable wife."

Yehoyaqim still said nothing, but raised his tented eyebrows even higher.

Shimon continued his monologue.

"There are several young maidens in the village, of course, who have recently come of age.

"Really, for that matter, one is spoiled for choice; one cannot complain, at all!"

He gave a high pitched laugh.

Yehoyaqim at last gave him the slightest of nods.

Shimon's mouth opened, and then closed again. His lower lip trembled. He knew he was making a mess of this and felt his face would explode. *No doubt it looked as red as a beetroot.*

"Have you come for advice on any of the families, then, Shimon?" the old man ventured.

Shimon blinked at him, his jaw dropping in dismay.

"No, no, not at all!" he answered hurriedly.

Yehoyaqim resumed his exasperating silent appraisal of Shimon's face, who could not take this any longer.

"I have come to ask for your daughter's hand in marriage," he blurted out.

If the elderly gentleman was surprised at this, in no way did he show it. After what seemed like an eternity again, his reply came forth.

"Maryam has not long since come of age."

Shimon bit his lower lip, thought for a moment, then parried in a weak voice, "yes, true, but ... but it is still proper for me to ask for her hand, is it not? Rev Yehoyaqim?"

"Yes, Shimon, I suppose it is," the elderly gentleman re-assured him. "So why have you set your eye on her Shimon? Given, naturally, that *'one is so spoiled for choice?'*"

"Because she comes from a good family, is healthy and fair, and will bear me many children." Shimon's rapid response indicated that it had been well rehearsed. "And," he added brazenly, "she also has a devout and well-respected father."

The most fleeting of smiles appeared on Yehoyaqim's lips. He then nodded gravely in assent.

An interminable silence followed, and now it was Shimon's turn to raise his thin, mousy eyebrows in supplication for an answer.

And after what seemed like an eternity, one came forth.

"It really is a bit early for her, unexpected too, as you well know. How fast children grow, do they not? Why not wait a while, Shimon?"

Shimon's jaw dropped once more. This time it seemed as if it took an effort for him to raise it to a close again.

"I ... I can wait ... of course!" he stuttered. "However, I, I just wanted to be the first one to ask ... you understand, apart ... apart from being the best one, hopefully, of course, for your daughter, I mean. The most suitable young man in the village, for sure!" Shimon then blinked rapidly at him as if to elicit assent for his claim.

"She is my first child to be married. Well, my only child for that matter," Yehoyaqim explained, "I have given no thought to matters of marriage, the choice of a husband, the dowry and all that, I mean."

"The dowry should be no problem for me," Shimon assured him eagerly. "If, if it's not too much, of course," he then added hastily. "So ... so is it alright, is it *'yes'*?

"Shimon. I have to think about it, discuss it with my wife and all," Yehoyaqim replied firmly.

"Yes, yes, certainly, I understand, of course, of course."

Yehoyaqim rose, but Shimon remained seated. The elderly gentleman frowned at this lack of respect.

"Rev Yehoyaqim," Shimon asked plaintively, looking up at him, "I *am* the first one to ask for her hand, am I not? And, and ... also, am I the only one?"

Yehoyaqim was still frowning down at him. Shimon suddenly realised he was still sitting, and stood up with a jerk. He then lowered his head and gazed at the floor. The carpet seemed a bit threadbare. He made a mental note of it.

"Yes, Shimon," Yehoyaqim assured him firmly. "Yes, you *are* the first, and seeing you are still here, obviously the only one," he added sagely.

"Good!" Shimon seemed to breathe a sigh of relief, which was not lost on Yehoyaqim, whose eyes narrowed.

"The only one, *so far*," Yehoyaqim then elaborated, tactfully.

Shimon froze, and Yehoyaqim smiled. "As I said, she is barely of age. It is too early for that sort of thing." He then patted the young man on the shoulder, and leaving his hand on it, led him to the door, which he opened with his other hand.

Shimon stepped out but turned swiftly back to face him.

"When shall—"

Yehoyaqim did not let him finish, "you will hear from me. In due course, Shimon, in due course. Good Evening!"

"Good evening, Rev Yehoyaqim," Shimon replied with all the respect he could muster.

The door closed gently, but firmly. Shimon stayed and stared at it, replaying the entire encounter in his mind and assessing his own performance. He gritted his teeth. He felt he really could have done much better. A wheezing laugh, one that was quickly transformed into a cough, fell on his ears from somewhere and shook him out of his thoughts. He twisted and looked up with a jerk to see the grinning, toothless face of old Ribqah at her window perch. He wagged an angry finger at her, was about to shout something up at her, but then thought the better of it.

Furious, head bowed to the ground, he tramped away.

CHAPTER TWELVE

With the hem of her dress scrunched in her grip, Maryam raced down the paved road that led down to the village well. She ran so fast, it looked as if her life depended on it. She skirted around other people, some of whom were heavily laden, trudging uphill, and others, lighter, going downhill to the well. All were carrying buckets and it was into one of these that the girl finally bumped, to send flying and clattering across the stony road.

"Hey, easy there, you silly wench!" yelled a tottering, red-shawled woman, whose bucket it was. Regaining her balance, she quickly set down her other bucket and chased after it as it rolled and gushed water all over the place.

"Sorry, sorry!" Maryam shouted over her shoulder as she kept going.

"Hey, there's been water in that well for centuries!" the woman screamed at her receding back, "it isn't as if it's all going to dry up today!"

But Maryam neither stopped nor replied.

An old man was grunting up the three wide steps that led up from the clearing in the valley in the middle of which the well was situated. He had two buckets slung across a pole on his shoulders and as he rocked from side to side with the effort, water sloshed out over the brims.

The spill made the mossy steps dangerously slippery and the moment Maryam stepped on the top one, she slid and went flying. Screaming, she braced herself for the fall on the hard stony ground.

It never came.

She fell right into a pair of steady arms that swung her away in a semi-circle, out and upwards from the ground. She looked up and gasped, as a huge, square, ruddy and bearded face grinned down at her. His shiny light-brown eyes were lights that smiled from deep under their bushy dark-brown brows.

Yosef!

Yosef was holding her in his arms like a baby: her long legs dangling over one sturdy arm, and her head lolling over the other.

"Maryam, are you in a hurry to see me, or what?" he laughed, raising his right arm to turn her head to face him.

"No, I'm not!" she lied, trying to sound indignant. "And put me down!"

Yosef started lowering her down.

"No wait, don't put me down, just yet," she corrected, smiling impishly. She beamed up at Yosef who looked back down at her, pleased. Then something caught his eye and jerking his head to the side, he frowned. Maryam twisted her head to see a woman close by, approaching them and giving them the weirdest of looks: the same woman whose bucket she had knocked over, apparently back at the well to refill it.

Under her messy red shawl, her eyes were like hot coals; one of these was heavily squinted. Her lips were pursed so tight they had gone white.

Yosef promptly lowered her down to her feet, gently.

Maryam gave him the widest of smiles. "Thank you, kind sir."

Her expression then quickly became serious, and she said, "Yes, I *am* in a hurry to see you."

She placed her hands firmly on her hips.

"Weren't you supposed to talk to Papa yesterday? You didn't! So ... *why didn't you?*"

"Well, I got caught up in Tverya, helping Shimon," Yosef replied.

"Shimon?" *Of all people?* Maryam could hardly believe her ears.

"Yes, Shimon, why? What's wrong with that?" And without waiting for her reply, Yosef briefly recounted what had occurred at the harbour in Tverya.

"Till what time, were you with him then?" Maryam enquired.

Yosef thought for a moment, "It must have been till the early evening. He paid me my wages and left me at his place to sort out the stuff we'd carried over. He must have taken off, for he wasn't at home when I'd finished. It was well after sunset by then and I thought it would not be proper to call on your father at so late an hour. It was strange for Shimon to trust me alone at his place, but he seemed to be in a hurry."

"I bet he was!" Maryam exclaimed, exasperated. "Well then, he must have rushed straight away to my house, to Papa; and you know what?"

Maryam did not wait for his answer.

"He went and asked him for my hand in marriage!"

"He did not?" Yosef's face was a study.

"Yes, he did!" Maryam yelled. "You didn't exactly expect him to inform you of his intentions, now did you?" Her voice had more than a trace of sarcasm.

"And ... what did your father reply?" Yosef asked nervously. Maryam was surprised, yet pleased to notice the way his hands fidgeted, the break and alarm in his voice.

"Well, thank God, Papa told him he needs time to think about it. He informed Mama and me about it later on that evening. You should have seen my face! I ... I tried to speak, but he would not let me. Later on, he went and talked with Mama alone about it after supper. They did not tell me what they finally decided."

Yosef stood there gloomily, at a loss, his arms crossed on his chest.

"Well, what are you waiting for?" Maryam screamed at him.

"What?" Yosef asked.

"What?" Maryam looked up and dramatically gazed at the sky as if to ask the Good Lord for forbearance. Then, bringing her head back down with a jolt, she jammed her face straight into his.

"Go, go now, *right now*, straight to Papa, and *you* ask him for my hand."

"Yes," he replied, "I will, I will ... only, just one moment." He grabbed the roped-hook to lower his bucket down the well.

Maryam's arm shot out and swept the bucket over into the well-mouth. It clattered down the sides until it hit the surface below with a huge splash.

Maryam peered down at it.

It was floating dismally on its side on the dark, rippling surface. She then felt eyes on her back, and spun round to see the woman still gazing at them, one hand gripping her bucket tightly, her other hand on her hip, apparently amazed at her antics.

"Go now!" Maryam screamed at Yosef, "*I* will fill your buckets! And even *carry* them up for you!"

The woman gasped as she heard this and, tilting her head to one side, cocked her good eye disapprovingly at her.

Yosef looked about to protest, but Maryam's flushed face and defiant glare cut him short. He spun round and, clearing the wet steps with a single bound, raced up the road to the village.

Maryam sat down with a sigh of relief on the rim of the well and looked over to the woman, who was still standing there like a statue, bucket and all, gazing at her. Maryam felt like making a funny face at her, but instead gave her a smile.

The woman did not smile back.

CHAPTER THIRTEEN

"Hannah!"

Hannah continued with her washing of the dishes. A few moments passed.

"Hannah!" The call was sterner now, and Hannah answered.

"What?" she asked over her shoulders.

"We need to speak."

"So speak," she replied insolently, turning back to the dishes.

"You stop whatever you are doing right now and come and sit here!" Yehoyaqim's tone of voice brooked no argument.

Hannah put down the metal pot she had been scrubbing with a bang, rinsed and dried her hands and went over.

"So tell me, what is it?" she asked, as if she did not know the answer already.

"I could not sleep last night, you know," came the reply.

"I know," she said with a tilt to her head and a grimace to her mouth. For really, given she slept next to him, his tossing and turning in bed all night made that comment quite superfluous.

"It's Maryam's betrothal, you see," her husband began.

"I know."

"As you know, I had decided to accept Shimon's suit. We both know he is very suitable for her, an upstanding member of the community, generous to the Synagogue both in service and material assistance; and he is reasonably wealthy, too."

He paused for breath, then added, "And he seems to be in love with her."

"I know."

"Yet, for some inexplicable reason, I just don't feel as good about it as I should."

"I know."

Yehoyaqim flipped at this point. "Hannah, can you say nothing else but '*I know*'?" he shouted at her. "If you know everything, then why on earth am I talking to you?"

"I *don't* know," she replied, irking him with her emphasis. She then decided to take it easier on him, and added, "Maybe you need my advice; if you would only let me give it."

"So, when did I stop you?" he sounded hurt.

"When you decided, by yourself, only yesterday, to accept his suit for a start!" she snapped.

Yehoyaqim stood and stretched out to his full height. "I am the head of the family, and it is for *me* to decide whom my daughter, my only child, marries!" he declared indignantly, pointing both index fingers at his inflated chest.

Hannah also stood, and without a word, turned and strode back to her kitchen sink, which was out in the back courtyard.

"You come straight back in here!" he bellowed at her receding back, "I'm not finished yet!"

Hannah was about to utter another '*I know*', but thought the better of it. So, instead, she retraced her steps and plopped back down on her seat.

"So tell me," he asked her once more, his tone more pleasant this time, "why do I not feel good about this?"

"*I?* ... Tell *you*?"

"Yes," he ordered. "*You* ... tell ... *me*!"

"All right," she replied with a sniff. "It seems to me you felt bad about this situation for two reasons, maybe three.

"One: despite all his attributes you sense there is something wrong with Shimon, something undesirable."

Yehoyaqim blinked.

"Two: you know that Maryam does not want him."

"Three: you also know perfectly well that *I* do not want him, *either*".

Yehoyaqim seemed infuriated at how simply she could put into a few words all that had been troubling him all night. Yet, he gritted his teeth and said nothing.

After a moment he shook his head in bewilderment.

"But it still makes no sense," he said exasperatingly.

"To a woman, an *arranged* marriage is what never made any sense," Hannah declared sagely.

Yehoyaqim glared at her. "That is our tradition," he growled between his teeth. "Would *women* now have us change our tradition?" he demanded sarcastically.

"I am not saying that a child should be free to marry whomsoever she fancies; I am simply saying that for a marriage to be successful, the child should at least have a say in it."

"You mean: she gets to choose her own husband?" Yehoyaqim asked incredulously.

"I said only that she should have a say in it. Do you not strive to take care of your family, to make us happy? And we are, thank God! So why should you not continue to do so, even in giving her away in marriage? That is your last act as a father with her under your roof, and it should be handled with the utmost care, for it is also the most important one."

It was clear that Hannah had touched him with this, for his face softened, his eyes widened, and he even blinked a couple of times.

"Choose?" he said after a while. "You said 'choose'; choose between whom? There is only Shimon so far ...?"

He was interrupted by a bang at the door, followed by another two in quick succession. Yehoyaqim's face clouded over again.

Hannah got up and hopped over to the door.

"Yosef!" she exclaimed upon seeing the young man, whose frame practically blocked the light through the door she had just opened.

"Good morning, Hannah. May I speak to Rev Yehoyaqim? Is he in?"

"Yes," she replied, a grin on her face; one which got wider and wider.

"Ye', it is Yosef, the carpenter," she called over to her husband, "he would like to speak to you."

"Now?" Yehoyaqim asked, irritated, "tell him to come back later, we have not finished yet."

Hannah surprised herself with her next action. Instead of doing his bidding, she jerked the door wide open, stepping aside.

The two men found themselves staring at each other.

"Rev Yehoyaqim," said Yosef, as he hesitantly stepped forward, "I need to speak with you. May I come in?"

Hannah turned, gave her husband a knowing smile and walked out into the back yard.

Yehoyaqim frowned at Yosef, was about to tell him that he was already in, but instead asked tiredly, "can it not wait, Yosef?"

"No, Rev Yehoyaqim, it cannot."

"Well, then come on in, I suppose," Yehoyaqim replied crossly.

Yosef closed the door behind him.

"Take a seat; you look hot, shall I get you a drink of water?" he offered. Yosef sat, but before he could reply, Hannah had already returned with two pewter tankards of water. She promptly went back out.

Yosef thanked him and, tilting his head up, gulped down all his water without stopping, his prominent Adam's apple jutting in and out of his red neck with each gulp. After he had drained it, he lowered his huge head to find Yehoyaqim, mouth agape, staring at him.

He put the empty tankard down and wiped his mouth on his other arm. "Sorry, Rev Yehoyaqim, but I was as thirsty as a camel!" The old gentleman softened his gaze, and the faintest of smiles crossed his face. Yosef, encouraged, went on, "Rev Yehoyaqim, I want to ask you for the hand of Maryam, your daughter."

Yehoyaqim gazed at him, and then everything started getting clearer in his mind. After what seemed like an eternity, he replied, "But she is barely a woman, Yosef."

"I know, Rev Yehoyaqim, but it is her that I want, and I wanted you to be at least informed of this. It may not be wise for me to wait any longer," he added with a tilt of his head to one side, and a knowing look in his eyes.

Yehoyaqim could not resist smiling openly.

"And what would you have to offer, Yosef?"

Yosef hesitated. "In terms of dowry, not much, I'm afraid. I was hoping that you would permit me to settle the full amount over time ..."

"*Over time?*" Yehoyaqim asked icily.

"Like Yaakov did for Rachel?" Yosef was pleased that he had remembered the tactic he had thought of and rehearsed on the way there.

Yehoyaqim was visibly impressed.

"So you shall work for me seven years?" he asked.

Both men smiled at each other.

"I shall work for you the rest of my life, if need be." Yosef's voice was in earnest. "I shall treat her well, protect and respect her, give her many children: make her happy, that I can promise you."

"Yosef, I need time to consider. I only have one daughter, as you know: no son. My seed can only be continued through her, so I must choose carefully."

Yosef nodded.

"Rev Yehoyaqim, as you probably know, I might not have much in the way of money at the moment, but although I may not be wealthy, I enjoy perfect health, thank God. And I am of the house of Dawid, I'll have you know."

"I know that, Yosef, as we are too, and that *is* important to me, very important," he assured the young man. Then he stood up.

Yosef took this to indicate that the meeting was over. He also got up, nodded and stepped over to the door. "I will promise you one other thing, Rev Yehoyaqim," he said, his hand on the door, "if, God willing, our first-born be a son, I shall call him Yehoyaqim, for you."

"Thank you, Yosef." Yehoyaqim sounded impressed at this, "as I said, however, I have to think about it." He closed the door and stood looking at it, lost in thought.

He did not know how long he had been gazing blankly when he gave a sudden start backwards as it was flung wide open again.

"Maryam!" he yelled. "You almost knocked me over! Is there no sense left in you, you silly girl?"

"Oh Papa, I am sorry truly! Forgive me!"

She smiled and hugged him.

"What were you doing behind that door? Were you on your way out?"

"No!" he replied crossly, "we had a visitor, I'd just let him out."

Yehoyaqim noticed that Maryam was beaming at him, and his eyes narrowed at her.

Then he heard his wife stepping back into the room. Glancing over his shoulder, he saw that she too had a wide smile on her face.

Maryam rushed over to her mother, who hugged her tightly.

Looking at them, he realised just how much his daughter had grown to resemble his beloved wife, and how close they were to each other.

Yehoyaqim understood, and thought for a while, till it was finally his turn to smile.

He then nodded to the two of them, —slowly at first, then resolutely.

CHAPTER FOURTEEN

"Ah," uttered Yosef, relieved.

The fierce afternoon sun had mercifully slipped behind a large dark grey cloud, and they were going to be spared its fierce rays for a while.

He was lying on his back on the sandy patch of beach next to the jetty at Tverya. Maryam lay supine beside him, a judicious distance away. Save for the heat, he was thoroughly enjoying their time there.

They had lain there for quite a while now, chatting profusely while looking up at the serene blue sky.

The couple had been formally betrothed the night before. Their first wish to celebrate this event had been with a trip to Yerushalayim, but Yehoyaqim had forbidden this out of hand.

So it was to the nearby fishing village on the Sea of Hagalil that they had opted to go to instead.

Needless to say, they were accompanied by the usual chaperone, which on this occasion took the form of Shelomit, Hannah's sister, who, despite being generally of a cheerful disposition, was keeping a very close eye on the young couple all the same.

She stood some distance off, talking to Zebadyah, a deeply sunburnt local fisherman.

Yosef's eyes narrowed as he realised that she seemed to like this rough tall, gaunt man, who, with his dishevelled, salt-speckled clothing, hardly seemed to be her type.

And he seems to be standing closer to her than he should, given that they are not related.

He grinned and jerked a finger in her direction.

"Hey Maryam, tell you what, it is *we* who should be chaperoning *her*!"

Maryam, who was twiddling her pearly white toes in the sand, as she lay fully stretched out on her back, giggled, her tiny tummy bouncing up and down. The movement was still visible despite the voluminous clothing she was wearing. In turn, Yosef gave his own belly laugh.

Shelomit seemed to sense she was the subject of their laughter and scowled at them. With a sniff, she then turned back to her heated discussion with Zebadyah.

"Maybe they're just arguing on the price of that dried fish," Maryam suggested with a chuckle.

Shelomit had bought from Zebedyah a sizeable amount of the much-renowned dried fish sold by the fishermen at Tverya—far in excess of what they really needed. They had had some of it for lunch on the beach, along with the bread, herbs and olive oil that they had brought with them. For dessert they had eaten dried figs and throughout the meal they drank red wine; and not a little of it. It seemed to have loosened everyone's tongue.

Over lunch, Yosef had recounted the incident of Shimon's overloaded ass, to the merriment of the two women. However, he wisely made no mention of the dark memory of that eventful day of many years ago that the trip had evoked in him.

"Maybe Auntie drank too much wine," Maryam whispered, still giggling, "she looks too red in the face to me. It can't be she's embarrassed or something, for Aunt Shelomit is never, ever shy."

Yosef laughed at this, "maybe I should have poured her even more wine!" He then added, somewhat hesitantly, "or poured *you* more." He looked at Maryam and almost winked. Maryam said nothing and Yosef, encouraged, ventured further—"maybe we can come to some form of agreement with her ..." His grin was saucier and wider than ever.

Maryam herself went red in the face at this, both her eyes and her stomach were fluttering, but she still said nothing. With a smile she gently reached out towards Yosef to find his hand already halfway towards her. She grasped it and gave it a squeeze.

It felt as rough and hard as any of the large pebbles she had tossed away from under her back when she lay down. She then rolled on her side towards him, and still blushing, hesitantly reached out and clasped her other hand to it.

He too then turned on his side to face her and caught her eyes admiring his chest, which now practically hid the rest of the beach from view. His eyes hungrily traced the graceful contours of her tall slim body. His breathing became heavier.

"How many children shall we have, Yosef?" she asked huskily. Although she was rested, she sounded short of breath.

"How many *boys* you mean?" Yosef corrected.

"At least three," he replied after thinking for a moment, "I would need three at least to help me with my work. I'm not sure I can afford to support more. For there are sure to be daughters as well, I suppose," he glumly concluded with an afterthought.

"Well, our daughters will serve to help *me!*" Maryam stated indignantly, letting go of his hand. He looked dismayed and she laughed. Reaching out again to pat it graciously, she declared, "We shall have a proper, enormous, hard-working household."

"We have to be very, very hard-working indeed if I am to afford all *your* girls' dowry." Yosef laughed.

"So I shall then give you as many of *your* boys as you need, Yosef," Maryam assured him gleefully, squirming to shift a bit closer to him. "And, what's more" she continued with emphasis, "our very first-born shall be a boy, I can feel it."

She paused as she thought for a moment.

"Yes," she eagerly resumed, "as the good book says, *the male that opens the womb shall be holy to the Lord!*"

"And pretty useful to me, too," Yosef quipped.

They both laughed aloud at this. Then Maryam squealed in pain as a fair-sized pebble hit and bounced off her hand. She shook it as her pinched flesh throbbed, and instinctively kissed the reddening bruise.

Spinning her head back, she scowled at Shelomit who had evidently thrown it at her from the handful that she had clasped, at the ready, to her abdomen.

"Hey!" Maryam screamed at her.

"Hey *you!*" Shelomit replied. "There's more where that came from, Maryam, I'm warning you! You keep your distance from him, girl! What in Heaven's name do you think you are doing? I shall certainly tell your father!"

Maryam giggled, knowing full well this threat was an idle one. However she obediently removed her hand from Yosef's.

"By God," Yosef laughed. He was on his chest now, gazing at Shelomit, head propped between his hands. "Your aunt is really an excellent shot. She could come in pretty useful should we ever finally revolt against the Romans!"

Maryam laughed, lay back and looked up at the sky, rubbing her hand. A thought seemed to strike her and she turned again to Yosef.

"Yosef"

"What?"

"What shall we call our first-born? His name; what name shall we give him? Shall it be Yosef ... for you? Would you like that?"

"No, no, not Yosef, not for me. Don't really want any confusion in my household."

Maryam thought for a while, then said, "Alright then, we'll call him for your father, Yaakov. What do you think, eh?"

Yosef's face took a serious turn.

"We cannot, Maryam," he told her after a moment.

"Why ever not?" Maryam asked, stunned.

"Because, well, how do I get to tell you this ...?" Yosef took his time. "I ... I, am not altogether sure who my own father is," he flatly stated.

"What!" Maryam yelled, sitting up abruptly.

Shelomit still had her eyes on them and she glared at Yosef. *Perhaps she was thinking he had said something improper to her ward.*

"Hey, calm down!" Yosef assured his betrothed, smiling. "It's the truth, I really *am* not sure, but these things *do* happen. However, in this case, there is nothing improper, you see," he added hastily. "Do not worry. My mother did nothing wrong and she was certainly no adulteress."

"But Yosef, if it is as you say, how can it be then? Go on, tell me ..."

"Well, it's like this," he started, "according to our tradition ..."

He gave a jolt as a bright flash stopped him in mid-sentence.

Then an enormous thunderclap crashed overhead, followed by a sharp gust of wind. They quickly scrambled to their feet in alarm. A thunderstorm had crept up unnoticed from the west and it started to pour.

On the hitherto calm blue sea, fierce gusts of wind began whipping the waves up into a frenzy, and sea spray was even reaching over to them as the rolling white crests broke on the shore.

Maryam shrieked, sprang up and covered her head more closely with her veil. Yosef grabbed her by the hand and rushed her to shelter in the doorway of an abandoned old fishing shack, which had an overhanging piece of flaxen sail stretched taut above it, over a frame of reeds.

Once they had reached the doorway, Yosef dutifully let go of her hand and stood gazing out in awe at the waves of sheeting rain sweeping over a sea that from its previous deep blue, had in minutes turned into a strange hue of grey.

"Yosef, go on, *tell me*," Maryam insisted.

"What?" he asked, eyes still fixed on the storm on the sea. He was worrying about the poor fishermen out there, who must be caught out in it. He prayed silently for their safety.

"About your father, I mean, how could it be that you are not sure who he is?

Yosef thought for a moment.

"Listen, I think I'd better have your father, Yehoyaqim, explain this to you. He is much more of an expert in these matters than I am; in our duties and traditions, I mean. Yes, it's better, for sure, I don't want to go wrong on this."

Although surprised at his answer, Maryam simply nodded.

"Speaking of whom," Yosef continued, seeming relieved that Maryam no longer insisted, "and regarding the name, do you want to know what I would like to call our son?

"What?" Maryam grinned at him.

"We shall name our first-born for your father!" he replied.

"Yehoyaqim?" asked Maryam in amazement.

"Yes, Yehoyaqim! Why, have you forgotten your own father's name?"

Yosef grinned saucily.

"But Yosef, it's too long a name!

"Why, I should go hoarse calling for him out of the window to stop playing and come to supper!

"'Yehoyaqim, Yehoyaqim!'" she quipped.

"Well, what does your mother call your father then?" asked Yosef irritated.

"She calls him "Ye'" for short."

"Well, we could do the same!" he stated flatly, "we'll just call him "Ye'!"

Maryam thought for a moment. Standing as close as she had ever been to the man she loved, she could feel the heat emanating from his body and smell the musty rain on his clothing. Her breathing quickened, along with her heartbeat. She fervently prayed he couldn't hear it thumping away. *'I'd do anything, for this man!'* she said to herself.

"Alright!" she told him, trying to sound not altogether pleased. "If that is what you want, I agree."

"Come on, Maryam, it's a great name," Yosef said soothingly. "Your father will be thrilled!"

Yosef beamed at her, happy that she had accepted his desire, without his having to tell her that he had already promised her father regarding the name. He wondered whether it was now safe for him to grab hold of her hand again, since he could feel it by his side. He remembered how warm and soft it had felt on the beach. Her skin was so fine and translucent that he remembered he could see and trace each tiny blue vein under it.

He gave a glance over her head to the side and thought the better of it; for although Shelomit herself was ensconced very close to Zebadyah in the doorway next to them, in the same way that they were, she was intensely watching their every move with a gimlet eye, and appeared not at all pleased at this turn of events.

The late winter thunderstorm soon passed over, however, and the sun winked back from behind the scudding grey and white clouds.

The rain soon faltered, pattered a little and then stopped as suddenly as it had started.

Shelomit bounded out into the street.

She strode right over to them as they stood still huddled close together in the shack's doorway, and waved them over towards the wagon.

"Come on, you two turtle doves. The outing is over, time to get back!"

Yosef could not help but notice however that Maryam's aunt was desperately trying to hide a smile, and her voice had acquired a soft undertone. The three of them bid Zebadyah goodbye, tossed the remaining dried fish and bread into the back of the wagon, and hopped on. With a sharp slap of the reins they were soon trundling on their way back up the hill to Nazaret.

YOSEF AND MARYAM

CHAPTER FIFTEEN

Dusk had ensconced the village within its dark mantel for quite some time when the two heavily shawled figures silently left their house and walked off, huddled close together.

The rustling of their clothes was the only thing to be heard in the quiet of the evening, as they made their way through serpentine alleys to arrive at a house in a corner. As one of them raised her hand to knock at the door, the other shot out her hand to stop her, saying, "Mama, I am going to speak to him alone!"

"Alone? At this hour? Are you mad? Impossible!" the older woman spat out as she raised her hand again.

"I said *Mother!*" The girl shook her mother's arm frantically away from the door. "*I am going to speak to him alone!*" she insisted, gritting her teeth and stressing every word. She went on, "it can only make matters worse for him, I mean, your being present."

"You are not going *in there* on your own, I tell you" argued her mother. "If necessary, I'll stay put in a corner, and not open my mouth."

Her daughter glared at her, eyes glinting in the pale, silvery light of a gibbous moon that shone overhead.

"Maybe even go to another room ...," the mother ventured.

Her daughter drew a deep breath through her teeth and with a cry of anger swiftly spun round and started walking back the way they came.

Her mother froze for a moment, then sped after her.

"Stop, stop!" she hissed in as loud a voice as she could allow herself. The girl however did not stop until her mother, reaching her shoulder, yanked her round to face her.

"Alright, alright. Have it your way! By God, my girl! You are as stubborn as your father! You go in and I'll stay outside, by the door. Do not take long though, mind you, for God's sake. You never know who might be watching."

They walked back to the doorway, and the daughter knocked gently. No answer. She knocked again, and yet again, each time louder than the last, yet to no avail. Finally her mother pounded at the door till finally they could hear footsteps. The door swung open. *'Only Yosef would have opened the door at this hour without first ascertaining who it is,'* thought Maryam.

He was glad and relieved to see them.

"Ah Maryam, Hannah, come on in!" He fairly beamed at them. "I thought you were never going to turn up, was getting worried about you again." He gave his betrothed an adoring look.

Maryam stepped in lightly, but Hannah remained outside. Yosef was stunned. "You're not coming in?" he asked.

Hannah shook her head, and bit her lower lip. Maryam gave her a nod and promptly closed the door. Yosef stared first at her, then at the door, perplexed; they had never been entirely alone inside with each other before, *ever.*

"This will not take long," she explained, "don't worry." She secretly hoped this to be so in her heart.

"It's alright Maryam, you can stay as long as you like, of course. You look better, much better than you did this morning. And ... sorry about the fuss I made at your house. Are you healed now?" Yosef raised his eyebrows questioningly, "is it over?"

Maryam looked at him, reddening, not quite knowing where to start.

'Yes, indeed, is it over' she wistfully pondered.

"I am not sick Yosef," she then told him, her voice slightly trembling.

"Good!" He grinned and brought his hands together with a resounding clap.

She blinked, then went on, her voice steadier now, "I was never actually sick, Yosef."

He gazed at her blankly.

"But this morning, and the days before, the throwing-up?"

"That is called morning sickness," she explained matter-of-factly. "Afterwards, I'm always alright for the remainder of the day."

Yosef blinked and frowned in thought. He tapped his foot on the floor, looking down at it while clearly trying decipher what she meant by this.

When he raised his head again, Maryam met his gaze.

Tears streamed down her red-rimmed eyes and onto her flushed cheeks, yet she made no sound.

Alarmed, he took her by the hand and looking questioningly into her eyes, sat her down gently next to him on a wooden bench. He held on to her hands and gave them a loving squeeze. Through her tears, she looked deeply back into his troubled eyes.

"What is it Maryam, tell me, why on earth are you weeping? What have I done now?"

"You have done nothing, Yosef." Her voice was trembling again. She gritted her teeth. 'Indeed,' she said to herself cynically.

She braced herself, inhaled sharply.

"Yosef, morning sickness is what women go through when they are with child!"

Again, he gave her a blank look. After some moments, he wrinkled his nose and asked timidly, "and in your case?"

"In my case?" Maryam gave a bitter smile, braced herself and went on, "in my case it is no exception: I am with child."

Yosef's jaw fell. Dropping her hands as if they were hot coals, he shook his large head and tugged nervously at his beard. He rose from his chair, shaking, and then sat down again.

Yosef gazed at her in utter amazement, sizing her up and down. He tried to search for something on her person, in the way she looked to make him believe what he just heard—in vain. The moment felt like a dream. She was looking straight back at him. Her eyes confirmed it. *It is real.*

He just could not believe it: she never averted her eyes, did not even look down, appear guilty or ashamed in any way. She was just sad; very sad.

Whereas he felt sick, and hurt, and angry all at the same time. His heart was pounding, his knees *even trembling*, and he was thankful he was sitting down.

Then, ever so slowly, his anger started to mount and surface through the sea of amazement that engulfed him.

"Are you sure?" he asked in a weird and broken voice that did not like at all.

"Yes, Yosef. I am sure. I have not seen my blood for three months now, and the morning sickness confirms it. I also feel different, not like I've ever felt before ... I ..."

She jumped as Yosef sprang up suddenly and started backing away from her. His old booming voice was back, and it was angry: very angry. "Whose child is it Maryam? Why did you do this? Have you no shame? Have you gone mad?

Or were you"—he felt cold at the mere thought of it—"*raped?*"

Yosef did not wait for a reply, clutching desperately at this explanation, "by whom? Tell me! Tell me now!" he hissed through his teeth.

"Yosef," she replied in a tone so soft and sweet, that it sounded like spring-water flowing in some brook, "I know no man. No-one has ever touched me."

Yosef stared at her. Then he twisted his head away, as far as it could go, then back again to stare at her pallid, placid face. He searched every line, every feature, every curve of it.

She could not possibly be lying.

That was one thing he was definitely sure of.

The other was that if she were really pregnant, obviously someone must have lain with her. *Maybe as she slept, in the night, and somehow had no recollection? But how could that be possible? Or could it? He did not know much about these things; about women in general.*

"Wait! Was it when you were in Hebron, visiting your aunt, Elisheva?" Yosef made some mental calculations. "That's it! It must have been!" he shouted.

"At Elisheva's house," he began as his thoughts raced, *'yes that's it!'* He finished his question, "did they hold a feast, a celebration?"

"Yosef, Yes! They did. Yes, we did celebrate when her child was born, that following evening; of course, there were lots of guests. Elisheva had told no one of her condition before. And certainly no one had expected her to *ever* bear a child.

Everyone was extremely surprised and very happy for her."

"Who was it that gave you wine, strong-drink?"

"Yosef, I had one tankard, two at the most. What are you thinking?"

Yosef took a huge step towards her, his blood boiling; then several steps backwards until he knocked into a baton that had been leaning against his workbench. It clattered to the floor and he instinctively picked it up. Then he lunged towards her again; but Maryam just stood there: not moving, expressionless.

Slamming the wood into the palm of his huge hand, he snarled, "Maryam, you utter fool, someone must have gotten you drunk, then ..."

He rapped with the wood again, choking on his words, "then he got you senseless, then ..." Yosef could not bring himself to say the words.

Maryam turned red, then white. "Yosef! Are you mad?" she protested, "are you insane? No one got me drunk; nothing *happened* that night. I was entirely aware of everything at the celebration. Afterwards I helped with the clearing-up and simply went to bed ... and slept. There was no-one there, with me, I mean." Her voice was strident.

"You slept alone, in your room?"

"Yes, I did, as usual. Elisheva has no other children, remember? She and her husband are old, and their parents are a long-time dead. And all the other guests had left too."

"All?" he spat the word out like a dagger.

Yosef's gut twisted as he realised how she had never seen him this way before. Her face betrayed her fear. Then her anger came to the fore.

"Yes *all!*" she screamed out at him, holding her hands to her face. "Don't you think that had somebody touched me I would not know it? Not even had I drank a whole wineskin! I'd still know!"

"But in the night——" Yosef started.

"I slept the night, I'm telling you!" Maryam yelled.

Then more calmly, she tried to explain, "in the morning, I rose normally. Had ... had anyone *known* me I would have *felt* different. Don't you *think?*" she asked sarcastically. "Even had I been completely senseless the whole night, as you are trying to imply. And I was *not,* I tell you!" she shouted out again.

"And the bed-sheets, no trace?"

"Trace, trace of what?"

"Blood!"

"No, Yosef, no trace of blood! I am intact, even now, as a woman, I mean! And I am telling you, *I was alone!* All the time I was there, or anywhere else for that matter, I was never alone inside with any man. Hey! In my *entire life* I had never been alone indoors with any man!"

"You are alone with me now," Yosef reminded scathingly.

"Yes!" she spat out, then stumbled to find the right words, "now ... yes, this is the first time. I did that for you, I did not want Mother's presence to embarrass you."

"Your mother, *embarrass* me? No! *No!* It is *you* who embarrass me, Maryam!" His tone was harder than ever.

Maryam gave a jolt and gulped. She clasped her trembling hands to her neck, and started weeping. Then she sniffed, looked down and said meekly, "yes, Yosef, you are right, I do embarrass you by ... by being like this. That is true, I am sorry, very sorry," she sobbed.

"You know what could happen to you?" Yosef said quickly, thinking he was in some dream, that he was not really saying this, that this could not possibly happen, yet at the same time knowing he was there, very much awake and staring at her, "were I to denounce you, I mean?" He barely choked the ominous words out.

"Yes," she replied gravely. He searched for her eyes in vain.

"Yet you also know that I shall not."

"Yes, I know that too."

Yosef's anger started to mount again. "You know that I love you, that I want you, and so you take me for granted," he hissed.

"No Yosef, I do *not!*"

"You *don't?*" he yelled.

"I ... I mean," Maryam clarified, "take you for granted, I don't!"

"I made a mistake, Maryam: a huge mistake. I really am the doddering fool everyone takes me for."

Yosef snatched a handful of nails off the workbench and fiddled with them absent-mindedly.

"You didn't make any mistake, Yosef. What on earth are you saying? You're no fool ..."

Yosef's anger blew at this point.

"I am not? No? Behold my Maryam, my betrothed: pregnant before our marriage." He glared and pointed at her belly, trying to find some outward sign of her condition.

There was none. "*And it is not even my child!*" he yelled.

At this, Yosef angrily rammed a nail into the baton he was holding, with his bare fist.

Maryam gave a start at the rap of the huge nail on the wood.

"And ... we do not even know whose child it is!" He drove another nail into the wood.

"I could look at any man from now on, and wonder, is *this* the father of Maryam's child?" he hissed, ramming one more nail in.

"Or is it *that one*, that man over there?" he said bitterly, ramming another.

"Yosef." Weeping, Maryam held out her trembling arms to him, ivory palms upwards, slender fingers reaching out to touch him. "Yosef, I was ... I am ... innocent!"

"Innocent? Yes, innocent, maybe ... probably," he shouted back.

"Or maybe drunk!" He slammed a nail in again, "or insane." He slammed another.

"Or both!" He stressed this by driving in two nails at the same time. Then he took a deep breath, stopped and stared the baton.

It was bristling savagely with nails, some straight, others askew. It resembled some terrible battle mace. He looked at his right palm. It was torn and bleeding. In his anger he had not even felt any pain, but now he did.

He flung the baton at the wall in disgust, and looked round to face Maryam. She looked horrified.

Then they spun round to the sound of frantic banging at the door.

"Mama! Mama, it's alright. I'm alright," she called out hastily.

"Yes," Yosef told her bitterly. "You are alright. It is I who am not alright."

He bit his lower lip. "Leave now, Maryam."

Maryam shook her head in despair.

"Just leave me," he repeated, his voice broken and tired. "Go! See what you can do with your life."

He thought for a moment, then added bitterly, "and I shall see what I can do with mine."

"*I don't want to leave!*" Maryam shouted defiantly.

"What do you mean?" he demanded, not believing his ears yet again. "Are you really, completely, totally, *utterly* insane? *Of course* you have to leave, *and right now!*" he barked.

"No," she said, shaking her head frantically. "No, no, *no!*" Tears were profusely rolling down her cheeks again.

"You ... you do not seriously expect ... expect me to still marry you?" he gasped in disbelief, his voice now hardly above a whisper.

Maryam gave him a weak and tearful nod.

Yosef was about to shout his angry retort straight into her face, but something stopped him.

Despite his intense anguish, and the gravity of the situation, he simply could not resist being fascinated by the beauty of the face in front of him; especially the heavenly look of her eyes. Her tears seemed to have washed them so well that he could peer further than ever before into their fathomless depths.

His anger dissolved immediately. He felt madly in love with her, more than ever, madly wanting her.

Mad indeed. He shook the thought off rapidly. He trembled, and stepped back, feeling almost scared of her.

He, Yosef, who had never been scared of any man, felt impotent before her.

"Maryam: *that* I could not take," he muttered. "The betrothal is over; I am letting you go. I shall not say anything to anyone, you have no cause to worry. You have my word. And if someone insists to know ..."

For some reason Yosef thought of Shimon as he said this, and he clamped his gashed and swollen right hand into a juddering tight fist, wincing at the stabbing pain. Crimson drops of blood fell to the floor as he squeezed it even tighter.

Maryam trembled.

"Yosef wait ... let me speak ... there is something else I have to tell you ..."

"There is *nothing* else!" Yosef yelled at her, "nothing to speak about any more, *ever!*" Yosef's voice was as hard as rock. "*Just ... go ... away!*"

Maryam froze, her imploring eyes as big as saucers, trying to find and hold his. But he looked away, swivelling his head from side to side to avert them.

The banging on the door resumed frantically.

"Now!" he screamed, and although she jumped, she still would not, *it seemed could not,* move.

He jerked the door open behind her and slammed it against the wall with a bang. A large saw that had been hanging on a nail fell and clattered on the floor, its metal band twanging hideously. Its curved row of jagged teeth seemed to sneer mockingly at him from the floor.

He turned to see Hannah's white, terrified face looking imploringly at him from the threshold. Yosef wanted to push Maryam out through the doorway, and he lifted his huge palms to her face; but he just couldn't bring himself to even touch her.

Maryam would neither move forwards nor backwards: she was as if paralysed. Finally, her mother tugged at her shoulders and pulled her back, tottering, into the alley.

Hannah hugged her daughter tightly to her chest as she walked her off, trying to stifle the sound of her sobs within her deep, dark cloak. She whispered softly into her ear, "off to bed, my precious one. It's alright, it's over now. Over and done with. Take heart, rest my baby, we shall speak tomorrow."

Through the doorway, Yosef gave them a long, lingering look, then slammed the door shut again. He stared at it in disbelief for a while, then, for his first time since childhood, burst into tears.

YOSEF AND MARYAM

CHAPTER SIXTEEN

Only three months earlier, Maryam had fallen asleep in very different circumstances.

She woke up and blinked her eyes in surprise at the domed sky; *where was she?*

Remembering in a flash, she sat up. The young maiden shoved away the cauliflower that had rolled onto her face from the heap at the back of the cart. The jolting and jarring of the wagon on the rough road to Hebron had not sufficed to rouse her from her slumber, —but the bristly scrape of the cauliflower rubbing on her cheek certainly had.

"How much longer do we have to get there?" she feebly asked the old man in front of her, who sat in the driver's seat propped up behind two huge oxen.

"Not much," the farmer replied, "only 'bout five hours or so."

"Five hours! Not *much*?" Maryam whined. And she fell back with a sigh onto the pile of sacks that had been her bed for over the past ten hours now.

Looking up at the azure clear sky, the events of the day before went once again through her mind.

****

"Maryam!"
"Yes Mama, I'm coming!"

Maryam flew into the kitchen from the courtyard where she had been assiduously hanging up the washing.

"Are we going now?" she gasped breathlessly, "the washing is nearly all hung up to dry." She wiped her wet hands hurriedly on her apron.

"Going where?" Hannah enquired distractedly.

"Why, to see Yosef, of course, Mama*!" Maryam replied condescendingly, as if to a child.*

Ever since their betrothal, Maryam had insisted on seeing Yosef every single day, even if only for a few minutes. Her mother had grudgingly accepted. And since most of the time he could not visit them before nightfall, she would call on him instead while he was working, duly chaperoned by her mother.

"Yes, yes, don't we go every single day, young lady? But later: for now I have some very good news I must share with you!"

Hannah's face shone.

"What is it, Mama?" Maryam felt excited at noticing the beaming smile on her mother's face.

"Elisheva, my sister, is with child*!"*

"What? Aunt Elisheva! I don't believe it, she can't be!"

Hannah nodded, and confirmed, "yes, definitely!"

"But she is barren!"

"Well, young lady, I'll have you know that everyone is barren until they have their first child!"

"But she is old, very old: ancient*!" Maryam laughed.*

"She is not *that old," her mother hissed, "only ten years older than me, for God's sake! These young people of today!" she whined.*

"Yes, Mama, but still at that age she's definitely past ... well, past, child-bearing age!"

"Maryam, you seem to know a lot about child-bearing. Who have you been speaking to now?" her mother demanded severely.

"Oh. Just the girls Mama, you know; we ask mothers, sisters, aunties, anyone, and then compare notes." She giggled.

"Maryam, listen to me girl: from now on if you need to ask something about these things, please ask only me! God only knows what fantasies you girls probably concoct! And have them ask only their own mothers too!

"You hear?"

Maryam gave her mother a hug, and Hannah's smile reappeared.

"Alright Mama, but tell me, about Auntie Elisheva I mean, how can that be? Uncle Zechariah is also very old." She was about to say ancient but thought the better of it. She thought for a moment, then went on, "wait ... no, no! Sorry, I forgot; how foolish of me, with men it is always possible to have children, whatever their age."

"Not always, young girl!" her mother replied indignantly, "but in terms of old age, way beyond the capacity of any woman for sure."

"So, Mama, tell me, how could it be?"

Hannah frowned, then grimacing, said, "Sit down!"

Her voice had taken a hushed and mysterious tone. Alarmed at this rapid change of mood, Maryam obeyed right away. "What I am about to tell you, you must tell no-one! Especially the girls ... promise me!"

"I promise, Mama," Maryam replied eagerly, and then asked timidly, "Not ... not even Yosef?"

"No, not even Yosef!

"Alright then, Mama, I promise. Go on, tell me, how?"

Hannah hesitated once more, then started, "our family has been blessed. For it appears that several months ago, an Angel of the Lord appeared to Zechariah, at the Synagogue, as he was praying, and said to him, 'your wife will conceive!'"

Maryam stared at her mother: her eyes wide, mouth open in amazement.

"An Angel? To Uncle Zechariah? Our uncle? I don't believe it!"

"Well, neither did he!" Hannah replied cynically. "I ... I mean," she hastily corrected, "he did not believe what the Angel was telling him, that his wife would conceive, that is ..., despite his many prayers for exactly that to happen, over the years. The Angel obviously he saw, of course. I mean, he could hardly disbelieve his own eyes, now could he?"

Maryam's mouth was still hanging open in utter amazement.

"And, because he did not believe in the power of the Lord, do you know what happened to him?" Hannah went on in a grim tone of voice.

"What?" Maryam asked with bated breath. Many of the stories she had heard from her parents about God's wrath on the unbelieving flashed through her mind.

"He was struck dumb!" Hannah slapped her thighs in awe and dismay.

"What?" Maryam said incredulously.

"Yes dumb! Dumb as a door-post! There and then. Can't say a single word, can only mutter and mumble and gesticulate and write down directions and requests and replies and things."

Maryam remembered her voluble, didactic uncle who was a fiery and vociferous priest at the Synagogue, and almost burst out laughing. But the grave look on her mother's face stopped that in its tracks.

"They need help, you see, Maryam. There's just the two of them, both advanced in years; one now with child, the other dumb. They need lots *of help. We don't want her to lose that baby, for God's sake. So ..." Hannah looked fixedly at her daughter, and took a deep breath.*

"So?" Maryam asked with trepidation: she knew what was coming.

"So you have to go over there and help her!"

Maryam's eyes opened wide in fear.

"But I cannot, Mama!" she cried.

"What d'you mean, you cannot?*"*

"Why, they live miles away, way out over there in Hebron. So it's not as if I could come and go often. At all!"

Hannah pursed her lips.

Maryam kept on with her frantic outburst, "also, you and Papa only have me, too! I have chores to do here; you know how much I do every day."

She waved her arm towards the washing on the line in the courtyard, which gave a flutter in the wind as if to confirm.

Hannah crossed her arms resolutely.

"I will *do your chores, Maryam.* You must *go over to my sister's!"*

"But there is also ..."

"Yosef? Isn't it?" her mother prompted her.

"Yes, Yosef, we have to prepare for our marriage and ..."

"We will handle the preparations."

"Yes, but we also have to talk, Yosef and I. We talk every day, about our friends, our home, the village, our wedding, his work, the children we shall have ... "

"Maryam, listen to me child." Hannah's tone was kindlier now, "you have your whole life with him ahead of you. So believe me: you'll have plenty of time to talk!"

Maryam realised there was no way out, and her heart sank.

"Can't they find a local girl?" she asked dismally.

"They can't afford it. Why, poor Zechariah is not even able to do the service at the Synagogue anymore!"

Maryam felt pangs of guilt and pity upon being reminded of her uncle's sudden unfortunate disability. She gave a sigh.

"Listen, my girl, my sweetest," Hannah cupped Maryam's face in her hands, and looked endearingly into her daughter's misty eyes, "it is only till her child is delivered."

"Nine whole months, ten ... no! Mama! I can't!" Maryam cried.

"What nine months? No, no, Maryam, Elisheva is already six months pregnant, so that's only three months left. There! Not an eternity, my girl."

Maryam was relieved somewhat at this. After a long pause she said feebly, "Yes, Mama. Alright, I'll go."

"Good! You shall leave tomorrow, I've arranged with old Nethanel."

"The farmer?"

"Yes, as luck would have it, he was due to deliver a wagon-load of the harvest anyway to Yerushalayim tomorrow, and he will go further on to Hebron for us. We've arranged to pay him for the additional journey."

"What? Me alone with an old man, for hours on end?" Maryam protested.

"A very old Man, Maryam. And out in the open, for God's sake, it's perfectly safe. No-one will have anything to say about this! Why, he's so old, that I honestly hope he does not die on us before you get there!" Hannah gave a nervous laugh.

"Are you sure of all this?" Maryam did not share in her laughter.

"Yes I am. Your father and I have discussed it, and it's alright. And, believe me, if it's proper with him, it's proper with just about anyone *in our village. What's more he's awed at this miracle, as much as I am, and wants to help out too, in any way he can."*

The wagon gave a jolt and that confounded cauliflower tumbled once more onto Maryam's face. This time it bruised her eye. Yelling out in pain, she grabbed it and tossed it over the side.

"Hey!" Old Nethanel shouted, "What the hell d'you think you're doing? He strained at the reins to bring the heavy oxen to a slow halt.

"Sorry, sorry," Maryam cried out hastily. She hopped off the wagon and rushed over to retrieve the cauliflower that lay like some large accusing eye on the wayside. It was hardly bruised. She dusted it off and showed it to the glowering driver.

"It fell into my eye, see ..."

She pointed at her smarting red eye with her white slender finger.

The old man gave a toothless cackle.

"Well, 'tleast it served to get you up off your back! You're all the while asleep, young madam," he muttered, taking the cauliflower from her and tossing it back over his head onto the heap. "Why, you even dream all the time you're awake, too!"

Maryam blushed at this and, without a word, climbed back onto the wagon.

This time she sat up, with her back to the wooden slats on the side, eyeing the huge, overfilled basket of cauliflowers warily.

She cupped her smarting eye with one hand, to protect it from the sun's fierce rays, and with the other looked for a while at the countryside and the other carts, wagons and horses on the road.

Her thoughts eventually shifted, as they always did, back to her Yosef.

****

Yosef had looked tired, very tired, when they had called on him to inform him of her trip.

Although visibly dismayed, he did not put up much of a resistance to the news of his betrothed's unexpected and imminent departure. For he also marvelled at the circumstances around

Elisheva's pregnancy and wished her well. Hannah assured him that the marriage would take place within a few days of Maryam's return, at which he smiled joyfully and hugged first her, then Maryam.

The young couple held hands, went into the courtyard and embraced as Hannah looked judiciously away. After a while, she cleared her throat, looked back over her shoulders and gestured that it was time to go. She opened the door and pulling her blue shawl over her head, stepped out.

At the door, the couple paused to look deeply into each other's eyes again, this time with some sadness, until Maryam finally pulled her eyes away from his, and turned to leave. Both of them had this strange ominous feeling that things had changed somehow, that something was afoot.

Yosef gave a shrug as he gently closed the door, and walked pensively back to his workbench.

Hannah—seeing the troubled look on Maryam's face— quickly sought to console her. She gently shook her by the shoulders, "Come on, come on, my precious. Take heart, Maryam! It's not exactly the end of the world ..."

She then gave her daughter a knowing wink.

"After all, listen, absence makes the heart grow fonder, as they say. It really does."

Maryam gave her the briefest of nods, sighed and managed a weak smile.

YOSEF AND MARYAM

CHAPTER SEVENTEEN

Maryam awoke, startled: something had thudded into her forehead. Reaching up, she felt that pesky cauliflower again. *How in heaven's name could it have fallen back on my head again?* As she sat up and flicked it aside in disgust, she heard a loud cackle.

It came from old Nethanel, who was rocking backwards and forwards in mirth, holding his palms to his kidneys. When he finally paused, he sputtered, "hey, young'un, we're here! We've arrived. Get up! Or is the back of my wagon *that* comfortable?

"Why, I thought that if nuthin would wake you up, that there old cauliflower sure will!" He cackled again. Stepping towards her, he grabbed the cauliflower and shoved it to her chest.

"Here, you can have the damn thing. Take it to your aunt!"

Maryam eyed the battered and bruised vegetable warily but accepted it anyway, thanking him.

She then stiffly hopped off the back of the wagon and, looking around in the fading light, could just about make out the city gate as described to her by her father. She was to wait next to it. Nethanel, in keeping with his re-iterated, solemn promise to her parents, also waited with her.

It was quite a while before an old but very upright man in priest's robes finally strode out of the city gate and, spotting them, came straight over. He recognised Maryam and embraced her.

"Uncle Zechariah! How are you? How is Aunt Elisheva, tell me?" she asked him, forgetting his disability for the moment.

Zechariah nodded and smiled. Pointing to his lips, he shook his head. She sniffed, eyes wide, then nodded back her understanding. He nodded the old driver off, who gave him a decidedly leery look in exchange.

But then, assured by Maryam's clear recognition of her relative, Nethanel proceeded to offload her box from the wagon and hand it to the priest. He then took his leave of them, wheeled his oxen around with a shout, and drove them back the way he came.

Zechariah eyed the cauliflower that Maryam was holding with some interest. Maryam laughed and as they started walking, began telling him the story, noticing with a smile how her uncle kept his face turned towards her as they walked.

Dusk had fallen by the time they reached a very small house on the other side of the city, in a corner where two sides of its high walls met. She was surprised at this location, for she was of the impression that her aunt lived in a very large house right in the centre. She looked questioningly at her uncle.

He realised her concern and nodding, gave her a smile to re-assure her that it was the right place. He rubbed his finger and thumb, and she surmised that they must have had to rent out their larger house for some income. Also, possibly, he preferred his wife to bring the child to term away from everyone's eyes and idle chatter.

They entered the house, and she spotted her aunt sitting on a chair near the window, her embroidery in her lap.

"Aunt Elisheva, God bless you!" she cried out, breaking into a run.

Elisheva jumped. She put her hand quickly to her abdomen.

"Maryam, you're here! May the name of God be praised!"

Maryam embraced her aunt tightly.

Zechariah smiled and started up the stone steps with Maryam's box to the room that his wife had prepared for her.

"Place your hand here, Maryam," Elisheva said, directing the girl's hand to the side of her protruding belly.

Maryam gasped as she felt something kicking, pushing and rolling against her aunt's taut skin.

Then she caught Elisheva's eyes, took her hand and placed it on her own slender belly.

Maryam arched her eyebrows questioningly at her aunt.

Elisheva's eyes suddenly welled up with tears as she looked searchingly back into her niece's eyes.

Then she gasped as she understood. Her eyes misted over, and, rising from her seat, she said to Maryam, with a voice high and mighty, "blessed are you amongst us all, for blessed shall be the fruit of *your* womb!

"And that is why my babe leapt at the sound of your voice. It has never done that before!"

"But how can you know already, Aunt Elisheva? Of my condition? No one knows yet, not even my mother. And ... and you are not even shocked at this?

However, please let me explain first: it was on my last night in Nazaret ... I ... I had a vision ..."

"I do not know how I know, Maryam, I just know, and I am convinced that all of this is of God's will, in your case as much as it was in mine! But do tell me of this vision."

Maryam nodded rapidly and began again, "on my last night in Nazaret, before my departure, I could not fall asleep, however hard I tried. I tossed and turned in vain. It must have been the excitement of my forthcoming journey. I had to get some sleep, though, and as soon as possible, for we were to depart at the break of dawn, and the trip was going to be very long and arduous.

"At one moment I was dismayed, thinking dawn had already arrived, without my getting any sleep, for I saw light at the open doorway to my room.

"Only it wasn't dawn at all! I looked at my window, and the night was dark still. Why, I could even see a bright full moon through it. The patch of light in the doorway then started twisting, taking shape.

"It was a figure, a being of light, with sparkles that rippled on it, like tiny stars. It was amazingly beautiful: an Angel, just standing there, looking at me. Light was streaming out of it, like some bright candle. A glowing, white, softly pulsating light that did not hurt one's eyes, but instead made you want to see more; made you want it to shine even brighter.

"I know I screamed at first but I don't remember hearing myself. And I'm sure I didn't scream out of fear, for I was much more amazed than scared of it.

No one else in the house heard any sound either, at any rate. I was on my own with this being.

"But all the same I felt re-assured as I noticed that the look it was fixedly giving me was actually a kind and gentle one, and unbelievable as it may sound, it also seemed like a look of awe, of admiration too.

"And although I was in my undergarments, and in bed of all places, I still felt safe, very safe; and I felt no embarrassment, none whatsoever."

"Was it a man or a woman then?" Elisheva asked with bated breath.

"It was neither ... or perhaps it was both!" Maryam replied in wonder. "One could tell neither by its clothing, nor by the figure, nor the face, nor voice. If you thought it was a man, something about it would then indicate it was a woman. If you thought then that it was a woman, something would change to make it appear like a man."

Elisheva stared at her niece in awe, "what did it say?"

"Why," her niece replied excitedly, "the very same thing you've just said: *'blessed are you amongst women!'* It told me that I was favoured; that the Lord was with me.

"'Me ... *why me?'* I thought to myself. Then I really did start getting scared, unlike when I had first seen it."

"Did it approach you, touch you?" Elisheva asked eagerly.

"No, not at all. It just stood there in the doorway, then looked and looked and looked at me. By then, I was trembling like a leaf, I can tell you, and my teeth started chattering.

"But finally it said, in tones that sounded to me like music, *"don't be afraid!'*

"It then told me I would conceive in my womb!"

Maryam looked down at her small belly, "and that I shall give birth to a son, whom I was to call *'Yeshua'*. He is to become a great man, and people will call him the Son of the Highest, and God will give him the throne of our father, Dawid."

She stopped and tilting her head to one side, looked quizzically at her aunt.

"You can understand how amazed I was at all this. Yet, I must say I also felt very happy at the angel's words. For I knew I was right in choosing to marry Yosef, that our children would continue the blessed line of Dawid, *but I never expected my first-born to ever become King!*

"Then I asked him *'when this was to happen'* and he replied, *'before sunrise!'*"

Elisheva gasped. And Maryam, reddening, continued, "I was stunned and asked it straight away, as to how that could be, since I knew no man yet. I told it that I had just been betrothed but not yet married to Yosef."

Maryam bit her lip, inhaled sharply, and continued, "it then told me that my first-born, my son, my Yeshua *shall not* be conceived through Yosef!"

Elisheva blinked.

Maryam trembled as she continued, her voice rising in pitch.

"I stared and stared at the Angel. I felt light in the head and almost fainted. I wanted that Angel to just disappear; for all this to be just a dream. I wanted to jump out of bed and rush out of the room to my parents. But I couldn't, for it just stood there, *blocking the doorway!* At that moment I felt *really* scared of it.

"A thousand thoughts rushed through my head.

"I did not want to marry any King, what I wanted was just that simple carpenter whom I was madly in love with. We had succeeded in getting betrothed to each other.

"How could I leave him now, how could I be ordered to? He was all I ever wanted. How could this be *happening* to me?

"Then the Angel explained, *'No man will come upon you, Maryam.*

'The Holy Spirit will fall as a shadow on you and you will conceive. You have found so much favour with our Lord, that you will conceive and give birth to His Son.'"

"I stopped trembling at that point, Elisheva. I was somehow no longer afraid. I really do not know where my courage came from, all of a sudden.

"It was amazing!"

"I also understood I was expected to do nothing ... nothing whatsoever, you know, except ..."

"Except?" Elisheva asked barely audibly.

"Except ... except to accept," replied Maryam resolutely.

Elisheva raised her eyebrows and nodded rapidly, urging her to continue.

"And I did," Maryam said with determination. "I told that Angel, *'from this moment on, I am nothing but the maidservant of the Lord, let it be as you say.'*"

Maryam then sank to her knees, looked up to her aunt and burst into tears. She nested her head on Elisheva's knees, who patted it reassuringly. Elisheva gently removed Maryam's white shawl and tousled her hair to comfort her.

Through her sobs, Maryam explained, "before the Angel's visit I wanted nothing else but to bear Yosef's children. Nothing could have made me happier than to give him his first-born, make a proud father out of him. It is what I had promised him, what I looked forward to, what I wanted to do, *so much*."

"That can never be now. It is over. It is done. I know I am already with child, and somehow you know it too. After the Angel of Light had disappeared, I sat in bed just staring at that open, dark and empty doorway.

"Not long afterwards, as I looked through the window, I saw that the real dawn had started to break.

"Yet then, all at once, it went dark again, as if a shadow had crossed over the dawning sky. I got up and looked out of my window: *the moon was gone!* No stars either, utter darkness!

"So I rushed back to bed. I huddled under the bedclothes, for the air in the room had gone suddenly terribly cold.

"But inside me, somehow, I was feeling warm, very warm, almost hot. It was a strange but pleasant feeling. I felt lost in it, overwhelmed. I do not even know whether I fell asleep again or not. But the dawn came back after a while, I was wide awake ..."

Maryam stopped, pursed her lips, then said, "And I knew I had just seen that new morning no longer as a child, but as a woman!"

She gazed into empty space and went on, her voice trembling, "I know more than anyone that I did not betray my betrothed, my beloved Yosef. Yet I also know that I must disappoint him greatly. I have no idea how to break this to him when I go back. And ..."

Maryam bit her lower lip to stop it from trembling, "I don't know whether he will believe me.

"*Yet so it must be!*" she gasped.

Maryam rose to her feet, and straightened out to her full height. She towered over her aunt, who had remained seated.

Her voice was now firm, stately.

"My soul is now here only to magnify the Lord. I rejoice in His favour, in His exalting me from a lowly girl from the smallest of villages, to one whom everyone will call blessed.

"Holy is His name and He will show great mercy to all those who fear Him; and He will scatter the proud in the imagination of their hearts.

"He will exalt the lowly, like he has done with me, and topple the mighty from their thrones.

"He will fill the hungry and empty the rich.

"He has never failed to speak and show mercy to Yisrael, and to our seed since Abraham, and will do so forever."

Maryam's face glowed as she then inclined her head towards her aunt and taking hold of her hands, started lifting her up gently to her feet. But Elisheva sank to her knees, her hands trembling in Maryam's firm grasp.

"How can it be granted to me, that the mother of our Lord should come to see me, to serve me!" she exclaimed in a broken voice.

Maryam kissed her head. She pulled her aunt back up to her. They embraced tightly, and wept on each other's shoulders.

After a short while they heard footsteps approaching.

"It is Zechariah." Elisheva sniffed, wiping her tears with her shawl. She placed her trembling hand on her niece's shoulder, "come, come let us go into the kitchen for supper. The table is already laid. But my child, please, please do not mention any of this to my husband, for now."

She gently led Maryam through the stone archway, and into her tiny kitchen.

YOSEF AND MARYAM

CHAPTER EIGHTEEN

"Maryam!"

Maryam was startled and dropped her buckets. She had just reached the well and the last thing she expected at that moment was to hear Yosef's voice boom out of nowhere. She hadn't noticed him at all; he must have followed her there and waited until there was no one else around.

She gave him a quick, sidelong glance, then slowly bent over to pick them up again. Turning, she started walking slowly back the way she came, empty buckets dangling from her long slender arms.

"Maryam!" Yosef called out again, sounding painfully surprised as she walked right past him with her head bowed, and without stopping at all. "Stop!" he yelled after her, "hey, where d'you think you're going?"

Maryam stopped, then gave a shudder, after which she started walking hesitantly forward again. Her buckets, although still empty, felt twice as heavy.

Yosef stepped forward and laid a hand gently on her right shoulder. She froze, and then spun round to face him. Her eyes were red, and brimming with tears.

"What is it Yosef?" she asked in a tiny voice, "you know we cannot be close to each other, even though as far as I know, no-one yet knows that you have left me."

"There is no-one here, Maryam. Look!" Yosef replied softly, with a sweep of his arm, which she followed with her eyes.

"We have to talk urgently," he informed her.

Maryam looked back at him and blinked.

"Do you ... do you *now*, at least, want to let me tell you what happened to me ... first?" she asked, her voice barely above a whisper.

"Yes," he replied meekly.

"You did not give me a chance last time," she moaned.

"I did not *want* to know what happened, Maryam. Can't you see? Nothing you could have said would have made any difference to me, at that moment"

"And now ... now it will?" Her eyes repeated her question, echoing her hope. Then she looked down at her feet dismally, saying, "and ... and even if it doesn't, you will at least hear me out?"

"Yes."

"And will you believe me?"

"I'll try," he replied firmly as he took her arm and led her back to the well.

Maryam put her buckets down on the rim and they sat to either side of them, turning to face each other. She recounted what had happened to her on that night before her departure for Hebron.

He listened intently, gazing at her in awe, at times nodding vigorously. When she had finished, he sighed. "Maryam, let me tell you—that Angel, that very same Angel, appeared also to *me* last night!"

Maryam's eyes opened wide, then lit up. She breathed a heavy sigh of relief.

"He *did*?" she asked excitedly, "where?"

"At home ... well, he did not exactly appear, in a vision, I mean. I was asleep, you see. He appeared to me in a dream.

 I had not slept for three nights after you'd told me you were expecting a child. I was devastated at losing you, at your condition. I kept worrying of what would become of you.

"At times I wanted you back anyway; at others I was very angry at myself for even contemplating this.

"Mostly though, I just wanted you to go away, and, on one occasion ..."

He paused, and looked at the ground in shame.

"On one occasion, I even resolved to denounce you!

110

"But that was for some very brief moments," he added hastily with a wan smile.

"Well, last night I was very tired and I just dropped half-dead into the bed. In my clothes, sawdust and all," he grinned.

"And this great shining Angel appeared to me in my dream and he addressed me by name! He told me, *'Yosef':* I can still remember the exact words ..."

"What did he say?" Maryam asked with bated breath, "go on, tell me!"

"He said, *'do not be afraid to take Maryam for your wife, for that which is conceived in her is of the Holy Spirit.'*

"It is the same thing you've just told me! Don't you see?" Yosef exclaimed, his ruddy face shining.

Maryam nodded vigorously, grasping the brim of her bucket with both hands.

"It cannot be a co-incidence, can it?" he asked her anxiously, reaching over and grabbing hold of her hands, "it just cannot!"

Maryam shook her head happily. Her face shone. She wanted to hug him, but he had taken her hands into his and was pumping them up and down as he asked her, "tell me just one more thing, Maryam, did he tell you what to name your child?"

"Yes, he did!" Maryam replied right away. "I have had that name ringing in my ears and embedded in my heart ever since that moment!"

"What?" he asked excitedly, "tell me, what was the name?"

"*Yeshua!*"

Yosef let go of her hands, jumped to his feet and swept the bucket next to him clear off the rim, and down into the well. After some knocking about, the inevitable huge splash was heard.

Maryam looked down at her bucket in dismay.

Yosef cupped her cheeks in the huge palms of his hands and gently turned her head back to face him.

"Yes! Yeshua, Yeshua!" he told her, stooping to bring his own face right down to hers. "That is *exactly* the same name he told *me* to call the child when he is born!"

Now it was Maryam's turn to stand up in excitement. She put one hand to her heaving chest and extended the other to his. She pushed at him and asked, "You ... you mean to say ... you were also told to call him *Yeshua?*"

"Yes, I was, and I *will* call him Yeshua. *We* will call him Yeshua. I shall take you to wife, and be a father to him as if he were mine. No-one need ever know!"

Maryam gave a cry, fell back down with a bump onto the rim of the well, then rose up again. With a scream and a swing of her arm, she swept the remaining bucket into the well. They laughed as they heard it land on the other one with a huge rap. She hugged Yosef's neck tightly.

After a while, he gently removed her arms.

"Wait," he told her cautiously, "there might be other people around. We could be seen, it's not proper."

Maryam did not know whether he meant this or not. She searched his face, and they both laughed again.

He then proceeded to quickly fish out the two buckets with a length of rope and a hook, and having re-filled them, started carrying them up the road for her. Maryam hopped from one side of him to the other in glee, chattering away.

Yosef suddenly remembered something and stopped abruptly.

"Maryam, there was another thing the Angel told me," he declared solemnly, as he lowered the buckets to the ground for a moment. "He told me, *'Yeshua, your ...* "

"'Our *son'*," he quickly corrected, "*'will save the people from their sins'*

"Save them from their sins," he repeated blankly.

"How can a King save his people from their sins?" Maryam asked in wonder, "not even a High Priest can do that, surely? No man can."

"I do not know," Yosef replied, perturbed.

"Neither do I know *how* he will become a King, for that matter, as the Angel told me," Maryam said.

They walked a while longer, lost in thought, yet at the same time extremely happy at being together again.

As a young couple on the open road by themselves, they got quite a few strange looks from passers-by, and so the two made sure they kept a reasonable distance between each other. However, many apparently either knew or assumed that they were betrothed, and no one bothered them.

After a while, Maryam stopped walking. "Yosef," she announced gravely, "there is one other thing, you know ..."

"Yes, Maryam, what is it?"

"You ... I," Maryam blushed deeply, "we cannot ... um ... there must be no doubt, about his conception, I mean ..."

Yosef understood right away, but nodded to encourage her to finish what she wanted to say. This she did, haltingly: "you ... must not lay with me as your wife, until after he is born!"

She pursed her lips and raised her eyebrows to elicit his response.

"I understand, Maryam. I will not," he assured her.

"You are sure of all this Yosef? And you will not change your mind about marrying me? After a few days ... in future? And how about this abstinence?" Maryam was rapidly beset with a flood of doubts.

"I will not!" he reassured her, "neither on one nor on the other!"

And Maryam's heart sang as she beheld in those eyes of incredible strength of his, which had won her heart forever, that he absolutely meant it.

YOSEF AND MARYAM

CHAPTER NINETEEN

"Hear Ye! Hear Ye! Hear Ye!"

The loud summons rose above the early morning hubbub of the village square at Nazaret and by its third re-iteration, served to utterly silence it.

"Gather round, villagers, and hear the edict of His Imperial Majesty Augustus Caesar, Almighty Emperor of Rome and of the World!"

People thronged around the Roman centurion who was flanked by twelve soldiers. From his perch on a high stool he was swinging his large helmeted head from side to side, his haughty eye going over the crowd of people gathering around him.

Everyone seemed to want to get as close as possible to the huge centurion, and his twelve-man armed guard had a hard time keeping the crowd at bay.

Several hawkers had even left their stalls unattended to come over and listen. The priests and their helpers on the other hand had formed a small group on the steps of the Synagogue and were eyeing him warily, as though to state their view that nothing good ever came from Rome.

The centurion, narrowing his eyes, glared over the crowd at them in turn. He would actually have preferred to deliver his speech from the highest step of that Synagogue, the most prominent place in this square, rather than from atop this rickety stool he was perched upon. But his superior had specifically ordered him not to.

A riot had broken out in Hebron only the day before when they had attempted to do just that. And Rome wanted full compliance with the Census, and no further commotion in this most troublesome of its conquests.

The soldier eyed the crowd again, and satisfied after a while with its size, proceeded to unfurl a scroll and start reading.

"His Imperial Majesty, Augustus Caesar, has issued the following decree! A census of the world is to be held with immediate effect. It therefore behoves every man to go and be registered in the city, town or village of his birth.

"And this, without undue delay. Those who fail to do so by the end of this year will face certain and severe judgement!"

Maryam shook her husband's hand. "What is a Census?" she asked.

A few heads turned to look at her at the sound of her voice, which had broken the hush that had fallen as the Roman spoke.

Yosef placed a finger to his lips, as he saw the centurion frowning at her over the heads of the crowd.

Silence restored, the Roman continued, "so those of you born here, in Nazaret or its surroundings can be registered right now, right over there."

He pointed with the rolled-up scroll to an old and bent scribe, who had duly set up a small stool and table a few feet away from the soldiers, just below the Synagogue steps.

The scribe flashed a sheepish grin back at the crowd and nodded vigorously.

Many in the crowd gave him looks of dismay.

The centurion, sensing the cause, hastened to add, "And, at the behest of our gracious and most magnanimous Governor Quirinius, there shall be no payment whatsoever levied on the public for this registration."

A buzz of approval rose from the crowd.

"Hear ye therefore, all Roman subjects, the decree of His Imperial Majesty Augustus Caesar, Almighty Emperor of Rome and of the World, and take care to heed it."

As the centurion hopped off the stool, he joined his men to control the crowd as it moved bodily towards the scribe and practically engulfed him.

Yosef had not forgotten his wife's question.

He now answered it, "Maryam, I expect this census is for Rome to have a list of every man in the empire. I suppose one has to register personally so that they have proof, and not just reports, of everyone in the land."

"Oh," Maryam said, relieved. Like everyone else, she had a deep mistrust of Rome, but at least, this did not seem that bad to her.

Yosef, however, frowned. "Probably some new tax is in the offing," he said, his voice low, "they want to make sure no-one escapes their dragnet!"

Maryam nodded as he led her away from the square.

"So, aren't you going to be registered? I mean, while the scribe is here, like everyone else?" She pointed to the throng around the Roman guard which had been shifted, as it were, from the centurion onto the scribe.

"I am," he confirmed, "but not here in Nazaret, though. I was born in Bethlehem, you see."

"The city of Dawid," she said with a broad smile.

"Yes, the city of Dawid," he grinned back, and went on, "so we shall have to take a trip and go there. And it's best it should be very soon; not much time left till the end of this year, and you heard the Roman's warning."

"But Yosef, I am now very close to my ninth month already!" exclaimed Maryam in alarm, pointing at her very prominent belly.

"Then we should go without further delay," he said, then paused and thought for a while.

"The day after tomorrow, Maryam, what do you think?"

"How long will it take us to get there?" she asked with a tone of uncertainty.

"Well, we should get there in four or five days I should say," he replied. A sense of dread and worry stirred within him, but he took pains to hide this from her.

Maryam nodded. "So be it, then. I will start making preparations."

"And so shall I," Yosef said.

They bade farewell to each other and made their separate ways through the throng.

YOSEF AND MARYAM

CHAPTER TWENTY

The couple had been on the road for four days, and with each passing one Yosef became increasingly worried.

Maryam kept re-assuring him that her time was not that imminent; that they had at least a week or more. But on her face he could nonetheless see the worry she seemed desperately trying to hide, especially each time the wagon took a jolt that was heavier than usual on the bumpy road to Bethlehem. He rode beside her on his donkey, often reaching out to clasp her arm reassuringly.

For every night of their journey so far, he had made sure they rested well at an inn for the night, as the caravan they had joined had to stop in any case to rest the horses, mules and camels.

Most of their fellow travellers, however, slept under the open skies, huddled together under heavy blankets against the cold winter night. Most of them were also going to Bethlehem on this unexpected, and in many cases, unaffordable, trip just to register for the census. Yet, although it was wintertime, it had mercifully not rained on the trip so far.

The wagon gave a huge, abrupt jar. It swayed and juddered. Maryam gave a scream and held both hands to her lower abdomen.

"Stop!" Yosef bellowed to the driver. The driver reined in the horses and glanced over his shoulder, an argument at the ready. The rest of the caravan behind them also came to a halt. Yosef's size and disposition immediately deterred him, however, and he chose instead to bestow on the huge man astride the donkey a steely, questioning glare. One that Yosef ignored.

At that moment they had been passing through the village of Bethpage and people in the street stopped to look with interest at the halted caravan. Maryam had turned pale; her husband could see that her mouth was twisted and that a cold sweat had broken out on her face.

"Are you alright Maryam?" he asked her, anxiously.

For once she did not answer straight away.

"Maryam?" he enquired again alarmed, shaking her arm. He felt a cold sweat form in turn on his own forehead.

"Yosef, maybe ... maybe we should rest for a day, what do you think? Just one day ..., we could then catch up ..."

"Sure, sure, we can do that," he assured her, "don't worry, we no longer need the caravan. We can make it on our own to Bethlehem. It's only a day away, maybe even less at that."

Maryam gave a sigh of relief, and Yosef offloaded their bag. He then sought the caravan leader, paid him off and watched as the motley train of wagons, carts, camels and horses continued on its way. He asked two men sitting by the roadside for the location of the nearest inn. Then Yosef lifted Maryam bodily onto his donkey and they made their way there at an easy pace.

He did not sleep a wink that night, constantly monitoring the often-ragged breathing of his wife, as she tossed and turned.

At dawn they set off. Yosef gently lifted his wife onto the comfortable seat he had prepared on the back of the beast, and taking the reins, carefully led it out onto the road.

They made steady progress through the cold morning air, as he watched out in the gradually increasing light for the ruts and potholes that pockmarked the well-worn stone slabs of that Roman road.

Night had fallen by the time they finally got to Bethlehem. He made enquiries about an inn with an old woman they spied sitting under a fig tree, surrounded by open sacks of mint, anise, cumin and other spices. Although she gladly gave them directions, she expressed her doubts as to whether they could find room there, for a large number of travellers had arrived that same morning on the caravan, and had posed to her that same question.

And she was right. Visibly dismayed to disappoint them, the woman at the inn suggested however that they try the only other existing inn, situated on the city's far side, just beyond its outskirts.

When they got there, though, the old and tired innkeeper, who answered the door and let them in, informed them that her place was also full. Not a single room to spare. She said that she had turned several travellers away already, and that these poor souls had been left with no choice but to sleep outside.

"But we can't do that!" Yosef remarked, pointing to his wife's condition.

The innkeeper gave her a look of commiseration and defensively holding her palms upwards, told them that if they wanted they could stay at a shed of hers that she kept for her farm-animals.

Seeing the looks on their faces, she hastily assured them that it was as clean as it could be, that there was lots of fresh clean straw in there, and also that it was at least quite warm. She said she would give them plenty of blankets and sheets too, adding graciously that furthermore she would not be charging them anything for it.

Yosef was at first somewhat aghast at the mere thought of this, but Maryam had taken hold of his arm, and squeezing it, had nodded frantically.

After gathering under his arm the bundle of bedclothes that the innkeeper had fished out of a chest, Yosef held his lamp up high as they slowly made their way to the shed, which was situated at some distance from the inn. As they reached it, Maryam stopped and staggered. She held on to the doorpost and cried out in pain, her other hand pressed tightly to her groin.

"Yosef, I think it is time!" she gasped.

Yosef rushed back to the innkeeper who said she would send her boy to get the midwife right away. The boy was thrilled at being allowed to ride the man's donkey, so as to fetch the midwife quickly. Yosef lifted the skinny boy onto the donkey's back and shoved the reins into his tiny hands. The tiny rider slapped the animal's haunch and sped off.

He then rushed back to the shed to find his wife inside, sprawled over a bale of straw. With a grunt, Yosef frantically made a wide heap out of another bale and spread a spotless white sheet over it. Then, heart pounding, he very gently lifted his heavy wife and laid her on the sheet, covering her with a blue and white striped woollen blanket.

A chattering and chubby midwife soon appeared in the doorway, carrying a bundle in one hand and a stool in the other. She was huffing and puffing and very red in the face. The boy led the donkey that had carried her over back inside the shed. When she saw the woman lying on her back on the bed of straw, moaning and writhing in pain, with her husband gazing down at her in despair, she stopped talking and rushed over.

Kneeling beside her, she took Maryam's hand and patting her cheek gently, reassured her. Then, looking over her shoulder, she brusquely sent the boy to fetch a clean basin, towels and a bucket of hot water.

Meanwhile Yosef tethered the donkey next to a cow that was shifting its large dark eyes from one person to the other, its hot breath condensing like smoke in the cold winter air.

The midwife then proceeded to examine Maryam, who was moaning continuously now, while Yosef averted his gaze to look out of the window at the starry night. After a short while, she rose, tapped him on the shoulder and gave him a re-assuring nod.

The two of them then helped Maryam get up and sit on the low stool the midwife had placed against the wall of the shed. As directed by her, Yosef dug a small hole, the size of a bucket, just under the stool, which she then lined with a cotton towel.

Just moments after the boy had brought what was needed and duly sent away, Maryam screamed, arched her back and heaved. The midwife and Yosef were supporting her arms as she squatted over the hole. After a short while Yosef, nudged by the midwife, jerked his head to look upwards.

Maryam gave the loudest scream so far, and the baby was delivered.

The midwife got Yosef to support his wife on his own as she deftly severed the greyish umbilical cord with a knife she'd had him cauterise on the lamp flame only minutes before. She then tied up the two ends with some twine, and helped him lower her back down onto the low stool. The midwife quickly covered her.

"You can look down now," she told him.

A boy.

The midwife grinned in satisfaction, and after she lifted him up and showed him to his mother, made a quick examination of the newborn. She then nodded to each parent in turn.

The infant did not cry.

Holding the tiny baby upside down from his ankles with one hand, she slapped it deftly on the buttocks with the other.

Still, he did not cry. The midwife looked cross and slapped the baby once more, this time harder. Again, no cry came forth. She quickly put the baby's face to her cheeks to make sure he was breathing properly. Seeing that he was, she breathed a sigh of relief, then, setting her teeth, was about to slap it for the third time; but Yosef's fiery glare stopped her hand in mid-air. So she gave it a perfunctory light tap instead: still nothing.

With a shrug the midwife proceeded to wash the infant gently in the basin full of lukewarm water, the temperature of which she had carefully checked and re-checked with her pink plump elbow.

She then patted the newborn dry with a towel and wrapped it up in the snow-white swaddling cotton bands she had fished out from her bundle. Finally, the nodding and gurgling baby was handed over to Yosef.

"Congratulations, *Papa*!" she told him huskily.

"And may I say that your boy is a tough, stubborn one," she told him with a laugh.

Yosef lifted him high above his head and exclaimed, "Yeshua!"

"And he looks just like you," he heard her say.

Yosef's face twitched. Cradling the warm pink-faced baby gingerly in his arms, he gazed at him in wonder.

"Is he alright, is he whole, is he healthy?" Maryam's breathless, exhausted voice came over, as she recovered.

"Yes, yes, of course he is, my dear." the midwife assured her.

Yosef was still staring at the baby, whose eyes were rolling from side to side as if to survey the entire surroundings. And he almost involuntarily resisted as the midwife brusquely took the babe away again from his arms to hand it over, ever so gently this time, to the mother.

Maryam looked at the babe in wonder, as the sweat dried on her face.

"Come on!" the midwife said to her brusquely, "what are you waiting for?" Realising then that this must be the woman's first-born, she proceeded to unceremoniously expose Maryam's breast with one hand and shove the baby's face onto it with the other.

The baby sniffed, then, shuddering his head, suckled with ease as his parents gazed upon him in wonder. Maryam smiled warmly down at him. The animals tethered close by, also seemed to find great interest in the scene, with Yosef having to keep pushing their poking heads away each time they got too close. Both the donkey and the cow breathed heavily down upon them, yet he was not altogether displeased at the warmth this gave. Their breath condensed into white streams in the cold night air and glowed above the child in the light of the lamp.

Maryam, still exhausted, soon nodded off and as the newborn child finally shook his sleepy head away from the breast, the midwife gently took him away. Cradling his neck in her hand, she held him to her chest and patted him on his tiny back with the other until he burped. Then, tightening the swaddling, she tucked him in a manger she'd had Yosef clean out and stack with fresh straw.

Flicking her fingers at him to turn away, she went over to the still heavily breathing Maryam and set about washing her. After she'd finished, she whispered to him, "I'm ready, but let her rest a bit now."

The two sat facing each other on the bales of straw, with the midwife chattering non-stop and Yosef politely nodding at intervals. He was mostly silent, for he was very tired. Eyelids drooping, he sighed in relief and, leaning his head back against the wooden planks of the wall of the shed, dozed off.

CHAPTER TWENTY ONE

Yosef's head snapped upright at the sound of heavy footsteps outside the shed. He scrambled to his feet as one after the other, three grizzled and very tall shepherds poked their heads through the doorway.

A huge, silent, flock of sheep came to a halt behind them and started to lie down all around the shed.

"May we see the child?" asked one in a deep voice.

"Ah, news travels fast," said the chubby midwife, "now, who would look for a newborn baby in a cattle-shed? Eh?"

The shepherd squinted at her.

"Certainly, come in, come in," Yosef replied enthusiastically. In some strange way, that shed now felt like home to him. "The baby is resting now, though. Do not make too much noise, please."

The shepherds stepped gingerly in and knelt in a semi-circle on the floor. Their gaze at the tiny child sleeping in the manger joined that of the cow and donkey, both of which seemed to be transfixed by this newborn child.

"There was no room at the inn. That is why he was born here, you see," Yosef began apologetically.

"And the donkey, and that cow, they're keeping him warm with their breath ..."

The kindly smile he received from the shepherds after they gave looks to one another, swayed Yosef's embarrassment.

"Is it your first-born?" one of the other shepherds, who had deep-set piercing eyes, asked him.

He hesitated for the briefest of moments before replying, "Yes it is our first-born."

Then he asked in turn, "but tell me, how did you men know about the child? It was that skinny boy I suppose."

"What boy?" the shepherd asked without taking his eyes off the baby.

"The innkeeper's son."

The three shepherds exchanged silent glances once more.

"It was not a boy that told us," the third one replied gravely, pausing for a moment before adding, "you will not believe this, but an Angel appeared to us tonight, out there on the hills, told us to come and see it. Gave us a fright at first, I can assure you."

Cocking her eye at the shepherd, the midwife sniggered and slapped her fat thighs with her hands. "You are certainly right, *we do not believe you,*" she stated emphatically, with a high-pitched laugh. "It's been a cold night eh? Out there on the hills, under the open sky, with the flock and all, I mean. Good idea to have something to warm you up, eh? What do you say? And not a little of it too, why not? As much of the red stuff as one could strap onto a ram's back, he he he!"

The shepherd scowled at her as he reddened at this; for it was certainly true, as everyone knew, that they often drank wine to stave off the cold.

The first shepherd came to his rescue, his icy tone cutting her off in mid-laughter as he rose to his feet, towering above her.

"Midwife, there was more than one Angel, I will have you know," he declared "a host of Angels, there was, for your information."

Maryam and Yosef stared at him, then looked at each other. A smile appeared on their faces.

"The first Angel we saw told us that this newborn child would be a Saviour, the Christ of the Lord," the third shepherd said.

The second shepherd nodded, adding, "And the Angel was then joined by all the others and gave glory to the Lord and announced peace on Earth to men of goodwill."

Maryam continued to look in wonder at each of the shepherds in turn: men whose awed voices had a distinct ring of truth to them. She then stiffly rose to her feet and unsteadily walked over to look upon the sleeping child in the manger.

The midwife, on her part, continued to glare at the visitors, without even trying to hide her contempt. She gave a huff and the men countered her contemptuous sneer with looks of disgust.

After a while, they then got up, congratulated the new parents and, taking their leave, silently filed out to lead their flock away, back into the bitterly cold night.

"The Christ in a manger," scoffed the midwife, rolling her eyes and tilting her head upwards as if to survey the rafters.

Yosef was about to say something when they again heard footsteps at the door.

The midwife gave a scream when the large head of a lavishly dressed black man poked through a window.

"May we see the child?" he asked her in a foreign accent.

"Do let me introduce myself: my name is Balthazar, and I have travelled from far away in the East. Are you the mother, madam?"

The midwife's jaw dropped low, then even lower as, without waiting for a reply, the man stepped through the doorway, to be closely followed by no less than two other finely-dressed gentlemen, who introduced themselves as Gizbar and Melchyor.

Yosef overcame his initial shock, shot up and proceeded to nervously introduce himself and his wife, as well as the midwife.

Then, with a proud flourish, he waved them over towards the child.

The visitors stepped closer and knelt around the manger to look down at the child in wonder, whilst Yosef, Maryam and midwife in turn stared back at them in stony silence.

"Myrrh."

"Frankincense."

"Gold."—each one said in turn to Yosef as they handed their gifts over, with a flourish.

The midwife slumped back, bewildered, onto a bale of straw. Gaping, she kept shifting her eyes in turn from the child, to Maryam, to Yosef and to each of the three gentlemen in utter disbelief.

After some moments, she gave a shudder and a squeak, leapt to her feet and, visibly terrified, asked her leave of them, promising volubly that she would be back the first thing early next morning.

Yosef made to pay her, rummaging in his leather purse, but she refused, muttering, "Tomorrow, tomorrow," as she grabbed her bundle and sailed through the door.

Balthazar jumped up and rushed out after her. He stopped the terrified woman near the inn. As he pressed a large coin to her palm, he bade her in no uncertain tones not to tell anyone of their visit. She promised, nodding frantically. He then made her promise once more, lifting her chin with his bejewelled fingers to make her look directly into his eyes. She promised again and then looked down at her palm to stare in disbelief at the gold coin that lay there. Trembling, she nodded vigorously once more and Balthazar, satisfied, went back to the shed.

****

After they had knelt around the child for an hour or so, the three visitors congratulated the couple once again, and politely took their leave of them.

They then sought lodging at the inn. The Innkeeper was amazed at the unannounced appearance of the three gentlemen.

"Of course, of course, we have room," she told them. "That is, if it is acceptable for you three gentlemen to share the same room?" she then asked in trepidation. "It's my best room, and quite large," she assured them. The dark gentleman assented with a nod, and she beamed at him.

"Have a seat then please, gentlemen, just give me some time to prepare it!" She then rushed upstairs and unceremoniously bundled her protesting old husband out of their bedroom.

Later on that evening, after a swift but wholesome supper, despite her many enquiries, both subtle and direct, the three gentlemen would not divulge to her the reason for their visit to the city.

****

At cock-crow, Yosef awoke at the shake of his shoulder by Balthazar, who proceeded to tell him to be wary of Herod, the King of Yehudah, the province in which Bethlehem was situated, and to keep the baby's birth a secret, for its own safety.

An Angel had apparently directed him in this way in a dream that he had had that very same night. He told Yosef that should they decide to flee the country, he had a close friend of his they could stay with, nearby in Egypt. He then gave him directions to his place, and the three gentlemen left quietly so as not to rouse the still-sleeping mother and child.

It was still not yet sunrise and Yosef, still exhausted, fell back to sleep. He awoke abruptly once more, and after quickly rousing her, anxiously explained to a still half-asleep Maryam that they had to leave right away, for he had just had a dream confirming Balthazar's warning to him.

When the midwife returned early the next morning to the shed, she found it deserted, with only the cow looking back at her. She stepped over to the manger, and was pleased to find the payment for her services placed in the middle of it. She picked up the seven small coins and, with a shake of her head, walked out as if in a dream.

YOSEF AND MARYAM

CHAPTER TWENTY TWO

Maryam gave a start. There was the lightest of knocks at the door, but her sharp ears had picked it up. Laying the baby gently in its luxurious, suspended cot, she pulled her white cotton shawl across her chest and went to answer the door.

She had been nursing her child at her window seat, and thinking. Although he had a healthy appetite, and her flow of milk was sufficient, everyone kept pointing out to her that he still looked a bit too small for his age. Yet, granted this did annoy her somewhat, she was not overly worried. *That's because they see me as a large woman and expect the baby to be large, too,'* she thought, and then wistfully surmised, *'and they see how tall Yosef is as well.'*

Not a day had passed since his birth, that she did not think of what the baby would have looked like had he been her husband's. Nor a day when at some point she did not wish it. But she was also convinced that she had done the right thing in accepting the will of God.

Furthermore, as the circumstances around the child continued very much to indicate that he was in many ways special, the doubts she at times had were swiftly dispelled.

Her handmaiden was at the door.

"My lady, the master would like to speak with you and your husband this morning," she informed her.

"Tell him we shall be down presently," she replied, and closed the door gently.

Well, he is up early for a change. She smiled to herself. *I wonder what's up.*

Serga, Balthazar's friend, and the master of the mansion they had stayed in for the past few weeks, was notorious for never getting out of bed before noon. Everyone surmised that his night-time exertions with the sizeable harem he kept understandably depleted him of energy. Maryam and Yosef also agreed that his heavy drinking would not improve matters either.

As she washed, Maryam remembered the lavish welcome he had prepared for them, and how surprised they had been. Clearly, Balthazar thought very highly of the child and had made sure that his friend hosted them in the greatest of comfort. *And it is amazing, too, how fast time flies by when one is living in luxury.*

She towelled herself dry, got dressed, then roused Yosef who lay sprawled on the huge bed. He gave a grunt, turned over, and promptly went back to sleep. Maryam smiled as she looked down lovingly at him.

Trying to shake him awake again, she thought about the time her days of purification would be over, and she would finally be a proper wife to her beloved husband, and give him his first child.

Yosef grunted and slept.

She shook him again, harder this time, and his eyes sprang open.

"Yosef, wake up!" she said. "Serga wants to speak to us."

Yosef stood up with a jerk. "I must have overslept," he said. "What hour is it then?"

"No, no, you didn't, it is still early." She laughed. "It is our host who must have fallen out of bed this morning. Come on get up, get dressed!"

"Wait!" Yosef said, his face serious. "I've just had a very deep dream"

"Ah, then that's the reason why I could not get you to wake up."

"Maybe ..." His face was still serious.

"What was it?"

"The Angel appeared again to me!"

Maryam caught her breath, not knowing what to expect. She sat on the bed.

"He told me we must go back to the land of Yisrael."

"What?" Maryam cried out, and instinctively reached over and picked up her baby from his cot.

"No, no!" Yosef reassured her. "Don't worry. You see, he also told me that those who sought to kill our child are now dead."

Maryam hugged her baby closer to her chest.

"But Yosef, how can we be sure?"

Yosef frowned. "I am sure!" he replied forcefully.

"But we might get back there only to find him still alive. Maybe he was very sick, reportedly dead or something and has since recovered ..."

"What did he die of, anyway, were you told?"

"I do not know what he died of!" Yosef cried out in anger at her objections.

She went on, heedless. "But it's safe here, and Serga assured us time and again that we're not at all putting him out. He is extremely wealthy: it's obvious. And you do help out as much as you can on his estate and he appreciates it, really does—that I know as well. So what else do we need?"

"Maryam, we have believed and obeyed the Angel so far, both you and I. Why should we doubt him now?

"Has he ever been wrong?" he added, pointing to the baby at her breast.

Maryam sat down on the bed and burst into tears. The baby seemed to look up at her in shock and dismay, so she stopped abruptly with a sniff.

"Yes, that is true, Yosef," she sobbed. "I'm sorry, I'm the one who should know that more than anyone, after all. But I'm so scared for him," she added, cupping her hand to the back of the baby's head.

"Maryam, listen, I understand your fear of going back. Tell you what, we shall wait a while; it does no harm, after all."

Maryam looked relieved. He went on however, "but only till we have confirmation. This is just to set your mind at ease, alright?"

Maryam lowered her eyes.

"Do you agree?" Yosef insisted.

She nodded and got up, placed the baby in its cot and hugged her husband tightly.

Downstairs, Serga gave them his usual loud greeting, with arms wide-open and profuse bows.

With a flourish he bade them over to his lush red carpet, which had already been laid out with several silver platters of food.

They sat and took of the food he offered them.

After enquiring as to how they slept, and other pleasantries, he started, "you know, my friends, I was roused early this morning."

Yosef and Maryam exchanged a sidelong glance.

"Very early I must say," he added with a hurt look on his ruddy face, "a messenger arrived at dawn from Balthazar, you see, bearing good tidings."

Maryam and Yosef looked at him in expectation, although they had more than just a mere inkling of what was coming next.

"King Herod is dead!" he announced.

Maryam and Yosef smiled and nodded at each other.

"Is it certain?" Yosef asked, hardly able to believe he was receiving corroboration for his dream so soon.

"It is certain," Serga assured him, nodding his big turbaned head vigorously. "Apparently everyone is rejoicing in Yehudah, and all the surrounding area.

"Not least his son Archelaus, who always desired the throne," he added sardonically. "The news has travelled fast. Balthazar made sure we would know quickly, because he thinks you should return to the land of Yisrael without further delay."

"But what about his son, this ... this Archelaus?" Maryam asked hesitantly.

"No, no, do not worry, his son is not a problem. He was never on good terms with his father, and was known to disapprove of that crazy mass killing of the male infants around Bethlehem. He believed it turned the whole of Yehudah against his father, and from what I hear of it, it certainly did.

"Everyone is celebrating that tyrant's death, and that includes his own son, I suppose," Serga concluded with a grin.

"How did he die?" Yosef asked, intrigued.

"Well, apparently, his notoriously large harem was not enough for him." Serga chuckled.

Maryam and Yosef exchanged another sidelong glance, and they had difficulty hiding their mirth.

Serga seemed oblivious.

He went on, "apparently as he was being carried through Samaria, he saw this attractive woman walking down the road with a pitcher of water on her head, some widow or other. He ordered them to stop. His men, knowing his disposition, warned him before he even opened his mouth that she was a loose woman, and that she even serviced the Roman soldiers, and thus was particularly unclean. Yet, he still wanted her, he did not care, and he had her there and then, in his carriage.

"Within days, he contracted this terrible disease. The fever would not leave him and he died after the elapse of a few short weeks. And his putting her to death in some ritual of sorcery was of no help to him. No cure was forthcoming."

Serga again gave his sardonic smile, followed by a short bleating laugh.

"So you and Balthazar think it is safe for us to return?" Yosef asked him anxiously.

Serga replied with a question, "one thing only: tell me, can you confirm what you've told me before, that is, that when you registered for the census in Bethlehem, you did not mention that your wife was expecting a child?"

Yosef nodded.

"Are you positively sure of that?"

Yosef remembered how they had seen the scribe on the road that led out of the city, by the other inn, as they were leaving and he had quickly completed his registration. The scribe was flushed and in a hurry, and had not even looked at Maryam, who had remained on the donkey. He certainly could not have seen her tiny newborn child at her breast and under her cloak; and he would surely have asked about it had he seen it.

"Yes I am, I'm sure" Yosef confirmed.

Thinking, he then asked, "but what of the midwife? The innkeeper, and her son? Any one of them could have talked."

"No, no, rest assured," Serga replied. "Balthazar has made enquires. They did not say anything to King Herod's soldiers as they rampaged through Bethlehem, and will surely not say anything now for fear of retribution.

"Also," Serga rubbed his finger and thumb together, "their silence has been well bought and paid for."

Maryam and Yosef nodded.

"But," warned Serga, "you had better steer clear of the land of Yehudah for now. I very much doubt that Archelaus believes at all that he's in some way threatened by some pretender to the throne, like his father did, but all the same you'd be safer in your own town of Nazaret, in Hagalil, provided you also keep a low profile."

Yosef smiled. "Hmm, but my trade is that of a carpenter," he reminded him, "so I have to be out and about around the country, a lot of the time."

Serga smiled and nodded, "do not worry; there is something else in our favour, I am also told. That other Herod, Herod Antipas, ruler of Hagalil, has an extreme dislike for his brother Archelaus, and this far over and above any normal rivalry you might expect. They were originally very close to each other as children, but they fell out drastically later on.

"Apparently, when they grew up, Archelaus once beat Herod easily in a public duel and embarrassed him greatly. He has never forgiven him since, despite his having spared his life. So there is no danger of his doing his brother's bidding; quite the contrary in fact."

Maryam still looked uncertain. A thought seemed to strike Serga, and his dark brow furrowed. He looked Yosef straight in the eye.

"Hey, Yosef, don't get me wrong here. I am, of course, not sending you away. As God is my witness! You are free to stay for as long as you want; this is your home.

"But then, if I were you I would follow Balthazar's recommendation. I know I always have. I owe most of my wealth to his advice. He is the wisest man I know, and I trust him completely. "

"We shall leave without further delay," Yosef announced. He remembered his dream and thought *'someone I also trust wants me to go back, too.'*

"We shall make preparations for tomorrow," he declared.

"I will arrange everything for you," Serga said. "Leave it up to me!"

He promptly snapped his fingers. A tall, dark manservant appeared right away, and Serga began firing directions at him.

Yosef gave Maryam a warm smile, took her hand, and after they had thanked Serga and taken their leave him, led her upstairs.

CHAPTER TWENTY THREE

The heavy banging at the door broke the stillness of the Nazaret afternoon. Maryam rushed over and looked out of the topmost window of her mother's house to see who it was.

Yosef!

"Hey Yosef, I'm coming down. One moment!"

"No need to come down, Maryam. I'm in a hurry, it's not you that I want; just tell little Yeshua to come with me, now."

"Yeshua?"

"Yes, Yeshua!"

"But isn't he at home with you?"

Yosef stared blankly up at her for a moment. He blinked.

"Woman, now why on earth should I come all the way over here to get him if he were at home, or with me?" he hissed.

"Well," she snapped, "he is not here! All the other children are, though. Do you want little Yosef, or Yaakov instead, maybe?"

The couple had just returned from a trip to Yerushalayim for the Passover feast, and they had only taken their first-born, Yeshua, with them. All their other boys, Yosef, Yaakov, Yehudah and Shimon, as well as her little girl, Shelomit, had stayed in Nazaret with their grandmother.

"But where is Yeshua then, if he isn't here?" Yosef snapped back at her, "he left Yerushalayim with you!"

For as was customary with the Passover caravans, men and women travelled in separate groups, with small children in the care of their mothers.

But in the case of older boys, these at times were allowed to travel with their fathers.

"No, he wasn't with me at all," screamed Maryam, "what on earth gave you that idea? After all, he left the city with you, in your group with the other men!"

"No he didn't!" Yosef insisted.

"Then where is he? My God!" Maryam gasped, slapping her hands to her face.

"I don't know where he is!" Yosef yelled, waving his fist up at her, "why didn't you take proper care of him? Or am I supposed to take care of the children too, now? Don't I work hard enough?"

"I tell you, I thought he was with you!" Maryam yelled back down, her voice breaking.

"He ... was ... not!" Yosef punctuated each word with huge bangs on the door with his fist.

"I saw him with you, Maryam!" He pointed an accusing finger up at her.

"And I saw him with you!" she shouted down to him, not the least deterred by his fury.

"Well, he cannot be both with you and with me, now can he?" he asked her sarcastically, "unless we're all travelling together, and that's not possible on the Passover Caravan!"

Maryam shook her head in disbelief and alarm, and pondered his words, *'Or could he have been with us both, though we were separate? Nothing about that child of ours should really surprise us any more by now.'*

The door was suddenly flung open, giving Yosef a jolt. Maryam flew out and started tugging him by the arm. "Let's go back!" she urged him.

"What, to Yerushalayim?" he asked, stunned.

"Yes, he must be there still, in that huge city, all alone on his own." Maryam gasped. She had let go of his arm and was already halfway down the alley. Yosef reached out his hand and yelled after her, "stop, woman, wait, what if he is here after all, somewhere in Nazaret?"

"Here?" she screamed, stopping and raising her splayed-out fingers frantically to her flushed cheeks, "here where? You say he's not at home! He's not at my mother's! Where else could he be?"

She though for a moment, then added hopefully, "Unless he's maybe at the Synagogue?"

"No, he's not there. That's precisely where I just came from. The priest wanted me to bring the child to him in fact, wants to talk to him, and that's why I came to get him."

"Listen Yosef, I'll have my mother continue taking care of our children and my father organise a search for him here, in the village," she said swiftly. "He can start by making enquiries with all the others who were with us on the caravan. In the meantime we must waste no time and start our journey back to Yerushalayim. *Right away!*"

Yosef nodded and as Maryam rushed back into her mother's house, he sped home to prepare their wagon for the trip.

****

By the time their wagon left Nazaret, there was still no news of their boy. Although by now it was dusk, the road to Yerushalayim was still full of traffic of all kinds, as was to be expected after the end of Passover.

And as if they weren't sufficiently distraught, they invariably got disapproving glances each time they asked whoever they met on the road as to whether they had seen a twelve-year-old boy on his own. No one seemed to have.

Maryam was becoming increasingly agitated, and Yosef's face was grim and dusky in the flickering light of the dangling lamp, as he spurred his donkey determinedly on.

Her thoughts went back to around twelve years earlier; to the first time they had brought their child over to that city, after her days of purification were over.

He was her first-born, so he had to be presented at the Temple. Yosef had bought the finest pair of turtle doves he could find, to be sacrificed there. On the way she had shown them to the baby she was cradling in her arms, and they had cooed softly at him through their wicker cage. He had looked at them intently, almost kindly.

They had barely entered the Temple when she was given a fright: the oldest-looking man she had ever seen in her life had come staggering towards them, and had unceremoniously snatched the babe from her arms. The other people present had grinned at her amazement and informed her that the man's name was Shimeon, and that despite being very old, it was reputed he would not die before he saw the Messiah.

He had scrutinised the child and held him up high over his head in his frail trembling arms. His liver-spotted hands were shaking and she was very afraid he might drop him.

As she moved closer to him, just in case, Shimeon had then proceeded to give profuse blessings first to God, then to Yosef and next to her, repeatedly announcing that he had seen the light that was to bring revelation to the gentiles and glory to their nation. He had finally handed the baby back into her eager embrace, concluding gravely that he could now depart in peace.

Everyone had looked on in awe, and many people there had crowded around the child. Thoroughly embarrassed by all the attention, her husband had kept gently pushing the thronging crowd away, while she had pondered. 'So is my son, this tiny Yeshua in my arms, really the Messiah?'

Old Shimeon had sensed her doubts and gently rebuked her, wagging his bony index finger in her face. He had told her the child was destined for the rise and fall of many in Yisrael, and for a sign that would be spoken against.

She had become more confused at this and, seeing her bewilderment, the old man had become even more agitated.

She remembered his looking directly into her eyes, and how in no uncertain tones he had proceeded to warn her that a sword would pass through her soul also, so that the thoughts of many hearts should be revealed.

Well, I'm feeling that sword passing now. Maryam came back to the present with a grimace. *What if we never find him? And had Shimeon actually died after he had seen the child? Had he really?*

She felt a pang of guilt, and regretted having never asked.

Her spirits soon rose however at seeing Yosef intent on driving the donkey as fast as the pot-holed road permitted.

She continued to reminisce of the scene later on that day.

Shimeon had finally tottered out of the Temple door, visibly dazed and exhausted, only to be replaced by this other old person, a woman by the name of Hannah.

The woman had also made a great fuss over their son, speaking of redemption or something. The people, who were still milling around them, had told her that the old woman was a prophetess from the tribe of Asher: a widow so devout, she never left the Temple. Apparently, despite being married, she had chosen to remain a virgin for seven years after her wedding. She had smiled inwardly at hearing this, remembering how she too had chosen to remain a virgin after marriage, but in her case it was only for close to a year.

But this old Shimeon, now this Hannah, what was it that everyone was seeing in her child? Her strange child?

Maryam stood up to look over her husband's shoulder. Yerushalayim was still nowhere in sight. She slumped back onto her seat, dejected, and continued to ponder about her missing son.

He was different. Everybody knew he was different: his brothers and sisters, relatives, people at the village. He seemed to stand out, and because there was no one, apart from Yosef and her, who knew of any reason for him to stand out, their noticing this was important.

It was as if he occupied more space than his body required, as if he was surrounded by some invisible cocoon. And he was not big for a child of twelve: certainly not when one considered the fact that they stood out as the tallest couple in Nazaret. Even two of her other boys, Yosef and Yaakov, were already taller than him, and so was Shelomit, her third child, who was a full two years younger.

At a Passover celebration, some years back, Shimon had even once remarked with a smirk, "Hey Yosef, your son looks more like me than he does you." And if he expected an angry rebuke from Yosef, this did not materialise, although she had noticed that her husband had winced at the words.

Yeshua, aged only eight days, had not even cried at his circumcision! 'Not as much as a whimper,' her husband had told her, when he came back with the child cradled in his arms.

And the priest at Memphis who had performed the ceremony had not only been amazed, but had furthermore kept insisting that he could have almost sworn to having seen the baby smile instead.

How could that be? And at eight days of age? Impossible!

Her thoughts were broken by the sound of the donkey braying as it stumbled into a deep pot-hole unnoticed by Yosef. The wagon rocked and Maryam held on. The fright at realizing her little child was missing had exhausted her, yet quite a while had to pass before she finally fell into a troubled sleep.

It was well into the next day that the wagon came to a halt at their destination, jolting her awake. They had arrived at the same inn they had left only a couple of days before.

The innkeeper was surprised to see them back so soon, and asked Yosef whether they had left anything behind.

He was even more surprised at the cynical reply: "yes we have: *our son!*"

With a look of commiseration, he told them that the last time he had seen Yeshua was when he was with them, when they had left his place for the Temple.

Leaving their wagon in his care, they swiftly decided to look for their child separately, agreeing to meet up again at nightfall at the inn.

Maryam was the first to be back that evening. Extremely worried, she collapsed, exhausted, on the bench by the door. And her heart sank when as she spied her husband on the road, approaching alone.

They then decided to go and pray at the Temple, and also to seek the priest's help in organizing a search for the child.

Upon entering it, they could hardly believe their own eyes.

In the orange glow of a huge Menorah's seven candles, there stood the priest, and *sitting* right in front of him, was Yeshua.

The man and their boy, both flushed in the face, were arguing intensely; and they were surrounded by a group of several elders, who hushed, looked on in astonishment.

Maryam stood rooted to the spot at finally seeing him.

He had been there all the time! She gave a heavy sigh of relief, as did Yosef who took her hand and pressed it hard. They stood and stared.

The heated debate between the priest and Yeshua proceeded, interrupted at times by an elder with some pointed question, to which Yeshua would answer rapidly and effortlessly, without even turning his head.

Yosef and Maryam finally shook themselves out of their daze, and rushed over to the boy. They stopped behind the circle of elders, and looked down at their son over their heads. Although he had his back to them, Yeshua somehow sensed their presence. Turning round, he gave them a wide smile. The elders gave the rough, dishevelled couple alternate looks of awe and disbelief, and opened up to let them through.

Yosef nodded at them reverently, but Maryam ignored them completely and strode up to the boy.

"My son, why have you done this to us?" she screamed into his face. "Do you know that we have been anxiously looking for you for *over two days*? You're just a little boy, on your own here! We feared something might have happened to you! How could you do this to us?"

Yeshua simply smiled back at her, entirely unperturbed by her outburst.

"But why did you seek me?" he calmly demanded of her, head turned, and looking up at her from his seat, "did you not know that I must be about my father's business?"

The priest and elders turned to Yosef at these words, and gave him enquiring glances. He inhaled sharply, and reddening, bit his lower lip and shrugged his shoulders.

They then enquired of him, softly, almost reverently, his name and lineage, where he lived, his occupation, and so on. And they looked perturbed and decidedly confused at his replies. Still, they proceeded to gather round him, clapping his shoulder and volubly praising the child. They urged him to bring him over to Yerushalayim at each and every Passover. Yosef was not altogether sure he really wanted to do this, but he had nodded to them all the same.

Having been stunned into an embarrassed silence by her son's reply, Maryam snapped out of her daze and, shaking her head, grabbed the boy by the hand and jerked him to his feet from his plush seat. Without as much as taking her leave of anyone, she stormed out of the Temple, dragging him behind her.

Yosef looked at her receding back in astonishment, excused himself volubly with the priest and elders, and after obtaining their blessing, followed her pensively.

YOSEF AND MARYAM

CHAPTER TWENTY FOUR

"Maryam, it's useless! I can't sleep; I feel like I'm going out of my mind!"

Maryam gave a sigh, mumbled something, turned over and promptly went back to sleep.

Feeling the blood rush to his face, Yosef shook her roughly by the shoulder. "Wake up!" he said, "didn't you hear me?"

"Yes, my dear," Maryam replied tiredly, giving the widest of yawns.

"Well then, wake up! What are we going to do?"

"Don't worry Yosef. How many times do I have to tell you?"

"How can I not worry, and how can *you* not worry? *It's unbelievable!* If I didn't know how much you loved him, I would think you didn't care whether he ever came back or not."

"I do care, and he'll be back!" she replied firmly, "like the time when he was when he was only twelve, remember? That must have been, what, nine years ago? God how time flies; how fast children grow."

"Maryam," Yosef hissed, getting angry. He dragged her to a sitting position on the bed. Maryam gave a sigh and rubbed the sleep out of her eyes with her knuckles.

"It's been three days and three nights now," he went on, "something must have happened to him, something really serious. He wouldn't just take off and leave without telling anyone. He must be dead or imprisoned somewhere! He could be injured, down some pit, unable to move, and dying of thirst!"

"He is *alive* and well. Listen to me Yosef, will you? I would feel it if something were wrong with him. I'd *know*."

"Women!" Yosef spat the word out, "dreamers, day and night!"

"Well, you dream too, don't you?" she replied pointedly, "*strange* dreams, too, and many of them!"

Yosef winced.

Maryam regretted the words the minute they were out of her mouth.

She took his hand and squeezed it reassuringly.

"Look at me, Yosef! Do you think even for one moment that God gave us this child, in those unheard-of circumstances, and with all those prophesies about his future, just to have him disappear into thin air, with nothing at all having been accomplished?"

Yosef blinked.

She went on, "the angels, the shepherds and wise men at his birth; his miraculous escape from the murdering hands of King Herod, and what we were told by old Shimeon and Hannah at the Temple: all for nothing?"

Yosef gave her a reluctant nod; he felt his anger quickly dissolving.

Maryam gave him a kiss and a hug.

"He will be back. As I keep telling you, just think of that time when he was lost as a child, when we found him at the Temple? Don't worry, take heart! Just pray for him to be back soon."

"Have *you* prayed?" he asked.

"No."

"Why not?"

"Because I know that he must have left for a reason; I trust in God. When it is time for him to return, he will return."

"So why should *I* pray?"

"Because you are not sure of his safety, so pray that his return will be soon."

"How *can* I be sure that he is safe? He left our *entire* flock of sheep on the eastern hill, unattended, without telling anyone. It's a good thing the ram stayed put, and so we did not lose them. And it was a miracle they were not stolen, nor attacked by wolves."

"He must have had to leave in a hurry," Maryam said.

"Or he could have been snatched, murdered and buried somewhere!"

"But whatever for, Yosef? He had no money on him, as far as I know, and as you say the flock was intact."

"Let me tell you what for," her husband replied ominously. "There are many over here that are jealous of his wisdom, of his goodness, of his popularity."

The barest flicker of doubt crossed Maryam's face as her husband spoke, "powerful people too, even at the Synagogue itself."

"But he is so good, he has never hurt a fly ..." she protested.

"Since when was that a defence?" Yosef snapped, "and listen, it's not only me who is worried about his sudden disappearance; it's all our children: Yosef, Yaakov, the other boys and the girls, they're all extremely worried. I know that for a fact, though they try very hard not to show us."

"I know that too, Yosef. I've gone practically hoarse trying to reassure them, and to stop them wasting so much time on the hills looking for him."

"The whole village knows he's missing by now," said Yosef sullenly. "No-one's really surprised, though; they all know how strange he is."

"Strange but good."

"Yes, strange but good."

"Come on, try to get some sleep now, my love," Maryam said, giving his arm a loving shake at the shoulder.

"I'll try Maryam, but, I'm telling you, I'm praying too."

"Yes, Yosef, my love, do that." Maryam gave him a kiss and slid back down under the bedclothes.

****

Maryam turned and stared at the wall, trying to sleep.

But the seed of doubt, the possibility of her son's coming to grief, had now been finally sown in her by her husband, and would not let her sleep.

After mumbling a brief prayer, Yosef had fallen asleep like a stone. *'It's like we're taking turns at keeping watch,'* Maryam thought with a wry smile.

She awoke suddenly to their dog's barking and frantic whining.

Yosef was still sound asleep and snoring. Maryam was about to shake him awake, when she jumped as the door of their bedroom was flung open with a crash. It was Shimon, her youngest son.

"Shimon!" Maryam screamed, "you gave me the fright of my life! What d'you want? And how many times have I told you to knock ..."

But the little boy would not let her finish.

"Mama, it's Yeshua! I saw him coming. I was out on the roof."

"Yeshua? You, out on the roof by yourself, in the dark? Are you mad?" Then she added anxiously, "Are you sure?"

"Yes Mama, and my eyes are *always* right, you know that!"

Maryam threw her bedclothes aside and leapt out of bed. Shimon had eyes like a hawk, and had many times proved to his disbelieving brothers that he could see much farther and clearer than any of them.

She was already halfway to the door when she remembered her husband. Rushing back, she gave him a shove so hard, he nearly fell out of bed.

Yosef woke up with a grunt. "Hey, what is it? What hour is it?" he grumbled.

"It's dawn. Get up quick, I think Yeshua is back!"

"Yeshua!" Yosef yelled, jumping out of bed. He then saw little Shimon. "Hey, what are you doing up my child, and why are you in here? Didn't we tell you you're not allowed in here whenever—"

"But Papa," Shimon's plaintive voice whined in protest. "It was me, I'm the one who saw him coming. I was up on the roof!"

"What! By yourself, at night?"

"I heard the dog whining, getting all excited, before dawn. It woke me up. I knew it was because of Yeshua. We climbed up to the roof. I was careful, don't worry Papa. I held my palm to the wall up the steps as you always tell me to. We looked, and the dog saw him at the same time that I did, and started barking. He was still far away, very far away."

"Alright, alright," Yosef said, getting dressed hurriedly.

He raced up to the roof-top to join Maryam who was already there, squinting at the distance. The dawning light was still dim, but a figure could definitely be made out, far off against the hills, and he seemed to be striding directly towards them.

"Is it him, Yosef, is it really him?" Maryam asked anxiously, hugging herself and trembling in the cold air of dawn.

Yosef peered into the distance, eyes narrowing.

"I can't make him out, but ... same height, compared to that hut over there, and yes, it does look like his walk."

"It's definitely his walk! You're right!" Maryam screamed and clapped her hands together with delight.

Little Shimon was stamping his foot in frustration at not being believed outright, as usual.

"His head seems strange, though. Surely it can't be him?" Maryam's voice was sinking, "it's big, but ... could it be a hood, maybe? Or could it be my nephew Yohanan instead, coming over to our house?" she added in dismay.

Yosef squinted.

"Yes, you're right, it does seem too big ... like mine," he chuckled, then went on, "no, that's no hood ... hold on. That's a scarf, that's a thick scarf he has wrapped around his neck!"

"It's not a scarf!" little Shimon's sullen voice floated up again.

They looked down at their youngest child.

"Well, what is it then, my little man?" Maryam asked him with a wide grin, her hands on her hips.

"Won't tell," Shimon replied sulkily, pouting his red lips.

Yosef gave a belly laugh, "alright, alright, have it your way, my little proud man. We'll find out in due course, as he gets closer, in any case."

Maryam saw it first. "Hey it's white; it's a white woollen scarf."

"Yes!" Yosef agreed.

"No it isn't!" Little Shimon was giggling now.

His parents pursed their lips, but they didn't ask him to tell them what it could be instead.

Finally, as the sun rose higher in the sky, and the figure striding steadily towards them came closer, Maryam gave a scream, and clapped her hands to her face.

"My God, it's a lamb, *a lamb*!"

"He has a lamb draped around his neck. It's not a skin, it's alive, I can see its ears moving! There, to the left, can you see?"

"Oh my God," Yosef said, with a clap of his hands, "that's it! Now I know! I did think for a moment that the flock we found was not quite complete: had forgotten all about that new lamb! We all forgot! But then, it's Yeshua's job to take care of the flock. The others have their work cut out for them, with the trade, and the field."

"Come on!" Maryam yelled in glee. She rushed down the stone steps to the courtyard, closely followed by Yosef who had picked little Shimon up in his arms.

They found the dog whining and scratching at the door; the other children had also started sleepily coming out of their rooms.

Soon they were all assembled outside the house.

When he arrived Yeshua lifted the lamb off his shoulders and lowered it gently into the sheepfold. Yosef ran over, and hugged and kissed him on the neck. Maryam and the children rushed to embrace him too.

"I saw you first! I saw you first!" little Shimon shouted as he hopped about and tugged at his hand. Yeshua took him up in his arms and kissed him.

"Yeshua, so tell us, was that it? Did you take off just to look for that little lamb?" Maryam asked her son in a broken voice.

Yeshua smiled and nodded.

"But was it worth it, Yeshua?" Yaakov, his brother, protested. "I mean you left the rest of the flock unattended, in open country; what, nine heads in all? We could have lost all of them. And you almost killed us with worry ..."

"I could not let it perish," Yeshua stated softly, pointing to the lamb, which had nestled up to its visibly agitated mother, "rejoice with me, for I have found the one which was lost."

At the sound of his voice, the flock came over to the side of the fold where he stood, as if to concur. Maryam had tears in her eyes as, taking her son's hand, she ushered everyone inside.

Yosef halted abruptly, straightened up, and gave a thunderous clap with his hands.

"Come on, Maryam, my children. This is a cause for great celebration, for I feared he was dead, yet he's alive. He was lost and now is found.

"Shimon, quick, go bring him my cape for he's shivering; it is cold. Let's go in. And, what's more, we're going to have a feast! To celebrate!"

He paused for a moment, and then gave another resounding clap with his hands, "and I've made up my mind: I'm even going to slaughter the fattened calf. Yaakov, go get the knife ..."

Yaakov jumped at this and stared at his father in surprise. He opened his mouth to say something, but then slowly closed it again.

YOSEF AND MARYAM

CHAPTER TWENTY FIVE

"Thirty years, already! And may you have many more years to celebrate!" Yosef augured as he raised his cup of red wine to Yeshua.

The family was at table: a table that Yosef had had to enlarge more than once, as its size increased.

On by one, in order, from eldest to youngest, his other sons and daughters raised their own cups and cheered the first-born of the family for his birthday.

Maryam raised and drank from her own cup, then rushed over to hug his shoulders and kiss his head.

They had just finished a sumptuous dinner that she had painstakingly prepared, with the aid of her three daughters, for the occasion. Yosef had also given the five boys most of the afternoon off and they all looked very fresh and contented.

Yeshua looked calm, and even more pensive than ever. Nonetheless, he gave a loving smile and an appreciative nod to each and every one of them in return.

They all loved him greatly, albeit at times he scared them in some strange way. Yosef was well aware of how they repeatedly told themselves and each other that there was nothing wrong with him: that he was just different. But the thing was, everyone felt he was even more different than they could easily explain away.

Yeshua finally also slowly raised his own cup and looked at the red wine, lost in thought.

'He's not drinking,' Yosef noticed.

On the plates hardly a morsel was left of the lamb that had taken practically a whole day to roast over a low fire, and there was going to be nothing left over for the dog except for the bones.

Only Yeshua had not finished his food. But then, they had long been accustomed to that; accustomed to how gently he ate, as if his every bite was the last one he would get to have.

So they all rose and left him on his own. The boys chatted with their father as he refilled their eager cups with more of the excellent wine he had obtained from Qana for the occasion. The high voices of Maryam and the girls floated over the clatter of the dishes. Yeshua sat regally, alone, at the middle of the table, the most generous portion of the lamb still only half eaten on the plate before him, with the wine and bread to each side of it. He seemed to be in no hurry to finish.

"So, come on everyone," Yosef announced, "time for our walk!"

The family had long gotten used to this walk around the outskirts of Nazaret at the end of some special occasion, and so had most of the neighbours, some of whom had also started doing the very same thing.

With two parents and eight children, several of whom were at times accompanied by their wives and husbands, they formed quite a troupe.

Yaakov had once jibed that, without this walk, the meal would be very hard to digest, and to everyone's merriment, Maryam had pretended to raise her arm to slap him for his insolence.

On these walks, Yeshua, albeit the eldest, would invariably end up bringing up the rear.

"Ever the humble dreamer!" Yosef would often remark.

But this time he seemed to be taking even longer than usual with his food and everyone was glancing impatiently at the amount still left on his plate.

"Think you'll finish by midnight Ye'?" Yaakov jibed, finally.

Yeshua gave him a smile and continued eating unperturbed.

Yosef strode to the door, opened it, and beckoned his namesake, his second-eldest, over, "Yosef, my son, you take charge. Go on, Yeshua and I shall catch up with you lot later. Wait for us at the steps of the Synagogue if we're late."

Yosef nodded.

He was visibly pleased at being placed in charge of the whole family, which was unusual. For he was much like his father, the quiet type, and quite unlike his younger brother Yaakov, who always seemed to have something to say, and who often took the lead.

He took his mother's arm and proudly led everyone out into the moonlit alley. A fresh breeze had come up, and Maryam and the girls pulled their shawls closer to their faces.

His father closed the door gently behind them and turned to look at Yeshua. He was still sitting quietly, almost as if he had not even noticed that the family had left for their walk without him.

"Yeshua, Yeshua, Yeshua," he said to him, slowly, resignedly.

Yeshua looked up, and stopped eating.

"What shall become of you, boy?" Yosef asked him, shaking his head from side to side.

"You have turned thirty. You still have no family of your own; you show no interest in my trade, no interest in finding a wife. What shall become of you?" he asked again, dropping into the chair opposite him with a heavy sigh.

"Of course, I will continue to support you, whatever you do. Even as you wander about and dream: practically all day long, and hardly do any work. Your brothers do not seem to mind either. I have never heard them complain, and that is surprising in itself because our work is indeed hard.

"But I shall not last forever, you know, my boy. I am already not as strong as I was."

He inadvertently placed a palm to his lower back as he said this.

"You have to see what to do with yourself, Ye'. You hear me? You have to think about your future. You can hardly expect your brothers and sisters to continue to support you, after I'm gone. They'll all have families of their own, as you well know."

Yeshua gave Yosef a benign, almost condescending smile.

In a sudden flash of rage, Yosef sprang up, shoving his chair back. It toppled over with a crash. "You just sit there and say nothing!" he shouted.

Yeshua hardly batted an eyelid.

Yosef shook his large head again in despair.

"My God, you *scare* me!

"How shall you fill your stomach? By looking at sparrows in the air and lilies in the field, for hours on end? Don't you understand I will not be able to provide for you once I am old and frail? Or dead?! Where shall you rest your head?

"Where will you find the means? Even to barely survive?

"I do not know what you are, but you are certainly no King, although you do walk like one; and talk like one.

"When you choose to talk, that is," he cynically added.

Yosef straightened up and his next words came out slowly, and sadly, "all I know for sure is that you are the son of my wife."

Yeshua's eyebrows seemed to arch just a little at this, or was it his imagination? He wasn't sure whether the words had inadvertently slipped out of his mouth, or whether he had really wanted them to come out. In any case, he decided to go flat out now.

"You are not my son," he declared, dropping his shoulders with a heavy sigh, and looking at Yeshua squarely. He did not really expect any surprise to show on Yeshua's face, and none was forthcoming.

Yet was that a slight misting in his eyes? Yosef could not be sure. He gave him a grave nod.

"Yes, I know that somehow you always knew that, but a time had to come when I had to state it out to you," he quickly explained.

"But then you should also know very well ... that had you been my own, I could not have loved you more than I did, or tried harder to teach you all that I knew, as any real father would."

Yosef sat down again and reached his arms over the table-top towards Yeshua.

"Yet, this was all in vain, it seems. Or am I wrong?

"You know some people at the village even say that you are Shimon's son!

"Not to my face, of course!" he then growled, punching a fist into his open palm, "but honestly now, who can blame them? Certainly your wit and easy speech come closer to his.

"And your size," he added with a hint of a sneer. "Yet, I do not believe that he is your father, not in the very least. Do not worry. All the same, undeniably, it really is clear to everyone around here that you do not resemble me the least bit.

"I have had to live with that all these years now. Thirty years old, and still half my size, however much your mother tries to cram into your stomach."

Yosef grinned as he pointed to the large amount of food still left on Yeshua's plate.

"But you are nevertheless strong: no one dares confront you. Already as a child you were so. So from where does your strength derive, I wonder? I know well enough that you have no demon inside you! Why, all the children, infants, even babes-in-arms smile at you, and animals are drawn to you, too. So evil cannot be within you. Hardly anyone like that in the village, except ... except maybe for that Eleazar, your only close friend. But then again, he is as strange as you are.

"You'd make a good shepherd, should you only choose to. But even there you seem to have lost interest: our flock has diminished instead of increasing. You choose just to read and dream and wander."

Yosef rose up, and started pacing about.

"Yeshua, tell me, what more is expected of me? Am I in your way? Should I depart now that you have grown up? Am I holding you back somehow, in some way?

"The Angel told me in that dream that you are of the Holy Spirit of God. Well, what else does this Spirit want of me? I am denied my acknowledged first-born; my seed has not flourished in the proper manner.

"My God has been hard on me, too hard!" He sighed.

"Even my own parentage is in doubt—still is. There are many, here in Nazaret, who know that.

You know that my Uncle Yaakov married my mother, his own brother Heli's widow, after his sudden death. She had not yet born Heli a single child, so as his brother, he was obliged to generate children for him through her, as is the custom.

"But of course," Yosef turned sarcastic, "even that was not enough. The heavens decreed also that I had to be conceived immediately and born prematurely: so tiny in fact that people wondered how I survived at all.

"What else? The perfect conditions for the eternal doubt to be created as to whom of the two brothers was my actual father."

Yosef raised his palms in despair.

"Try as she could my mother could not even tell for sure by my looks, for her two husbands had also looked so much like each other! As one would mostly expect of brothers, after all! And yes, I do know that it is all the same proper and acceptable to the Community; it is the law of Yibbum or something.

"But what about *me*? Is it acceptable to me not to know who my own father was? What are these games that God chooses to play on us?

"And later on in my life? I am betrothed to the woman I love. Then lo and behold! *You* come along: a further generation of doubt, of insecurity! Do *you* know who your father is? Or should I say *what* he really is? Will you ever see him?

"Why do you just sit there and say nothing? Is all that I have said not *important* to you? Do you *care* at all?" Yosef yelled, enraged.

"Ha," he slammed his fist into his palm again, "I realise, now, why you show no interest in having children of your own; perhaps you don't want to go down the road I went. I don't blame you at all, given our family history!"

Yosef clasped his forehead.

"For of course, having me go through life with an unknown father was not enough. God had to choose me again, ask me to marry a woman already with child. *Why me?* I am no priest, no sage, and no holy man: just a simple craftsman. Or is it my kind heart perhaps that He chose me for?

"Everyone tells me that my heart is even bigger than my head, and that is maybe true. For I know full well that I willingly accepted this intrusion into my life, this destruction of my dream of simply being the head of a normal, respectable, hard-working family."

Yeshua was still looking at him, without saying a single word. Yosef was increasingly feeling unnerved, but he went on.

"And your mother? Well, she accepted too, despite everything. Don't you think that she did not dearly want to bear for *me* my first-born? Have you any idea how deeply in love we were? Our marriage was not an arranged one. We both wanted only each other and in this we had succeeded. It was perfect; perfect until the Angel came calling, that is.

"She too said '*Yes*' to the Angel."

Yosef pointed his finger in anger at Yeshua, "but could she very well have said 'No'? Who can say 'No' to God? Say 'No' and expect to get away with it? Why is it always a sin to say 'No' to God? To ask that, for once, He maybe chooses someone else.

"Did your mother ever have regrets, do you think? Does she at times wish, even for a moment at least, that you were really *my* son and not His? I know I do. Do you ever think about this? I just cannot bring myself to ask her."

The unbroken silence on Yeshua's part then became intolerable.

"Say something!" Yosef screamed at the silent figure before him.

He glared into Yeshua's placid eyes and then tottered as a sudden dizzy spell washed over him. He held on to the opposite end of the table with both hands. Yosef could not take his eyes away from those of Yeshua. He was awestruck.

"Yeshua." Yosef's lowered voice now had a distinct tremble to it, "I know your eyes speak your replies. And they do not lie. There is no bottom to them. They go deeper and deeper, beyond anything anyone can ever fathom.

"But can you at least tell me of what you know; do I not at least deserve to know, too? What is the purpose of all this? What have you achieved? What is the meaning of all that talk of Light, Salvation, Kingdom? Or was everything just a strange bewildering dream?

"You have not even touched your wine!" he then snapped, stamping his foot hard, "the red wine I sought out especially for you! You make fun of us, I sometimes think! A stranger in our midst, in my own *home*. We are all of us but mere children before you!

"Well I am *not* your child," Yosef growled, straightening up with a jerk, and jabbing his finger again towards Yeshua, "your mother, your brothers and sisters share your blood, and they are blood-bound to you. But I am not, do you realise? Do you hear me?"

Yeshua remained immobile, silent.

"Still you say nothing!" Yosef's jaw dropped in dismay. Tired, he lowered his eyes, and nodding said, "I see, I see, it is I who is really the outsider here; the hired hand.

My left hand holds out the fruit basket to you and the axe I grasp in my right protects you. That is all. That's all that was ever required of me. Now I see ..." He tapped his right foot nervously on the floor for a while.

"But that's alright." Yosef was calmer now. "I said 'Yes', thirty years ago, and though I may falter, *I shall not fail.* I was never one to backtrack, as God is my witness. I have never taken a step backwards in my entire life."

Ironically as he said this, while still keeping his eyes locked on the straight-backed, silent figure sitting royally before him, he was inadvertently backing his way towards the door. As he struck it with his shoulders, he gave a start.

Yosef reached out behind him for the latch, opened and stepping out, spun round to slam the door shut, but instead, he closed it gently.

CHAPTER TWENTY SIX

"Aunt Elisheva! Hey, it's good to see you! Come right in! What brings you to Nazaret? We didn't know you were coming. Does Mama know?"

With these words, Maryam yanked the old woman, who was swaying and panting at her doorway, into her house and her tight embrace.

"One moment Maryam ... let me ... catch my breath," huffed Aunt Elisheva, pushing her niece aside to sink into an armchair close by.

"Let me get you a cup of water, Auntie!"

Maryam flew out into the courtyard. When she came back, she could see that her aunt had somewhat recovered.

"The wagon left me at your mother's ... at the other end of the city, you see, but ... there was no-one at home." Elisheva gasped. "So I turned back but he was gone, already, that idiot of a coachman!" She took a moment to catch her breath, "I didn't know where you lived and so I went round and round the city till I finally found this place."

She mopped her brow with her shawl.

"But why didn't you ask for directions, Auntie? Everyone knows where Yosef the carpenter lives!"

"Yes, but everyone is not telling, eh?" Elisheva replied, exasperated. A couple of passers-by I asked simply ignored me, and one even directed me to the *wrong* carpenter.

"To Shimon?"

"I don't know what his blessed name is. He's a bent, skinny guy, with straggly hair and a shaggy salt and pepper beard ..."

"That's him!"

"And a sneaky, lying cur of a man as well!"

"Why do you say that?"

"Well, I could see he wasn't pleased that I was asking for some other carpenter, and he directed me to an old abandoned workshop. Cats on the doorstep and a rat grinning at me from a high windowsill, in broad daylight! *Really!*" she gasped.

"Oh, he must have directed you to Yosef's old place." Maryam could not help but grin at this. "We don't live there anymore. But really, Shimon knows that for sure! He must have sent you to the wrong place on purpose!"

Elisheva wrinkled her nose in contempt, and then brightened up, "ah, so you have moved, to a larger place, I assume." She looked around with a smile. "Are you doing well then?"

"Not too badly, thank God, Auntie. And we also have a large family now. This new house of ours is bigger and closer to the road. It has a sizeable patch of arable land at the back, too. Come and see."

Elisheva got up and followed her niece to the open window.

At some distance behind the house she could see a large man leading a donkey that was pulling a plough through the hard, stubbly soil.

A young man walked behind, pushing and guiding the plough, as well as picking up and tossing to the boundary wall, the occasional unearthed rock; whilst another followed at some distance behind him, harrowing in the furrow with a hoe.

Maryam pointed them out with pride.

"That is my husband Yosef over there leading the donkey. The one driving the plough is Yaakov and the one a little further back of it is my second eldest, Yosef. Up on the hillside, those two boys with the goats and the sheep are my youngest sons, Yehudah and Shimon.

Elisheva squinted to make the boys out and smiled. "And Yeshua, where is he?" she asked.

Maryam looked but could not see him.

She frowned, and then her face lit up as a straight-backed man in a white tunic appeared from behind a tree.

"There he is!" she exclaimed, "he's the one sowing, behind the first two boys. He was hidden by that mustard tree for a moment."

Yeshua was striding confidently in the freshly ploughed furrow, into which he was dropping seeds at intervals from a sackcloth bag slung across his shoulders. At times, he stopped to yank out a weed here and there.

"What is he sowing, wheat?" Elisheva asked.

"I don't know, could be. I had a look at the sack of seeds this morning before they left for the field. They were very small seeds, extremely small; it is a wonder that they can grow into anything of much value. I shall ask Yosef upon their return, now that you mention it." She giggled apologetically, "I'm not at all familiar with farming; men's work, after all."

"My, your Yeshua strides like a King," Elisheva exclaimed, smiling. "You would not believe he was simply labouring in a field now, would you?

Maryam laughed, "Yes, Auntie that is exactly what everyone says of him. It is true." She thought for a moment, then asked her aunt, "and your Yohanan?"

Elisheva's face fell at the mention of her son's name. Maryam was alarmed.

"Why, what is it, Auntie? Is he all right? What's the matter, tell me?!"

Elisheva tugged nervously at her straggly grey hair.

"Yohanan is the reason for my trip over here," she replied sullenly. "He is alright. Healthy, I suppose, at least from the reports I get from time to time, though I can't honestly see how he can even survive out there."

"Reports? Out where?"

"In the desert!"

"In the desert?" Maryam's face went blank. Elisheva nodded. She looked sad, very sad.

"What is he doing there? Is he a soldier? A scout maybe?" Maryam asked, mystified.

"Soldier? No! Well, a warrior? Maybe! A warrior for God, perhaps," she quipped cynically. He has become a religious hermit Maryam. Just took off to the desert several weeks ago. One fine day he just removed his black robes and donned a cape of camel's hair, girdling it with a leather belt like some ruffian, some cave-dweller. They tell me he is some kind of prophet."

"But what does he eat?"

Elisheva made a face but, did not reply.

"Tell me!" Maryam insisted.

"They tell me he survives on wild honey, and *locusts!*"

Maryam cringed, "why is he out there?"

"He says he is doing God's work. Well, I must say, he has always been doing God's work for that matter, throughout his life. Very just and religious, always was. Everyone knows this. Doesn't even drink wine like your Yeshua. Was preparing for the priesthood. At Hebron everyone expected him to follow in his father's footsteps. Take up Zechariah's duties, in our division at the Synagogue, upon his retirement. But what does he do now that his father has retired?

"He decides to go off wandering in the desert, among thieves, the possessed, and even Lepers!

"The Synagogue cannot simply just wait for him, and he had an argument about this with his father. Zechariah forbade him to leave; got so excited he almost lost his voice again."

Maryam's eyes widened. "I see," she said. "I remember of that time, when he would not believe the Angel right away ..."

"Yes, he didn't believe, that is true, and it was when he remembered the consequences that he suddenly changed his mind and let my son leave.

"He even blessed him, in the end, as we saw him off, even though he had gone against his wishes and left us all alone, with no-one to support us in our old age."

Elisheva gave a whimper, "and I wanted grandchildren too, given that God had granted me a son. Was it too much to ask? Why does He demand so much of His people? The holier we are, the more He seems to expect of us."

A tear ran down her wrinkled cheek. She sniffed, and then straightened up, wiping it off brusquely with the back of her hand.

"Yet God works in mysterious ways, as they say," she declared, her voice trembling, "rarely can we see why he wants us to do the things he expects us to do. We simply just have to obey."

A thought then crossed her mind.

She turned to face her niece.

Looking at her straight in the eye, she asked, "but tell me one thing, Maryam: when the Angel gave you the astounding news, I mean, that you, a virgin, would conceive, did you believe right away?"

With heat creeping into her cheeks, Maryam thought back for a moment.

"Well, um, not exactly," she replied, "I simply put a question to it. I remember asking, *'how can that be?'*"

"But that is exactly how my own husband Zechariah reacted!" Elisheva exclaimed. "Yet in his case he was struck dumb. *You weren't!*" There was a hint of accusation in her tone of voice.

Maryam's face clouded over, her eyes saddened.

Her aunt reached out and shook her shoulder gently, smiling. "Come on Maryam, it is not as if I wish you had been, my dear, you know that very well I should hope! Silly girl! I am simply wondering why the distinction."

"I ... I suppose because your husband was a priest, and, and I was just a village girl ... and, perhaps, God made allowance in my favour for that."

Elisheva thought for a moment. "Yes, maybe," she paused, and then remarked, "no, that's not it! The truth was, I think, because my husband had been praying for years to father a child, and when his prayers were answered he did not believe it. So he showed no faith, no real faith, actually."

"Whereas I, in my case," Maryam stepped in eagerly, "I certainly didn't want to become pregnant before marriage, God forbid! All I wanted was to get married and build a normal family with the man that I loved."

"Yet, God had other plans," Elisheva stated.

"Yes he did, and I accepted that, though."

"And so, in my case, I to have to accept what he has planned for my special child, I suppose," Elisheva said resolutely. "After all He did put an end to my being reproached by everyone for being barren."

"Yes, and after all, one could hardly expect a normal outcome from very strange beginnings," Maryam concluded.

Elisheva looked at her niece at these words, and arched her eyebrows pointedly at her. Maryam understood her gesture right away and nodded.

"Yes," she replied, "and I know very well that that applies equally to my case. I was told that my first-born would be a King. Yet all I can say so far is that that is limited to the way he walks, and the way he talks, and the fact that everyone seems to obey him.

He always seems to have this warm glow about him too, draws everyone to him, especially children and animals. He is gentle yet strong. It is indeed strange: maybe it is a beginning of some future grandeur ...

"Who knows? We shall yet see. For I too want grandchildren of his, naturally, but so far he has not set his eyes on anyone, even though he has just turned thirty."

"Is it perhaps that no-one has caught his eye here in Nazaret?" her aunt ventured.

Maryam's eyes lit up in hope, "could be!" She paused for a moment, "no-one, that is, except perhaps for that young Maryam."

"Maryam who?" Elisheva asked, intrigued.

"Maryam, from Magdala, a neighbour of ours. A very beautiful woman, if somewhat wild. Yeshua is friends with her brother Eleazar you see. House of Dawid too: but it's nothing really, so far at least. They're just good friends.

"In a few months' time, though, we are all invited to a great wedding at Qana. Maybe he'll meet someone over there, who knows?"

She had moved back to the window and was trying to look out for Yeshua as she spoke about him.

But it was near dusk and a large cobalt-coloured cloud had blocked out the setting sun, making it difficult to make out the men in the distance. A chill fell on her.

She turned to face her aunt.

"But what if he chooses to do what Yohanan did?" she asked the old woman in trepidation.

"Would you accept?" asked Elisheva gently.

Maryam turned, stepped closer to her visitor, and looking straight into her face, answered without a moment's hesitation,

"Yes, I would."

Elisheva marvelled at the way Maryam's eyes lit up as she said this; with that same emerald fire that she had seen in them so many years ago, as she was relating to her the final words she had said to the Angel: her acceptance to conceive.

Encouraged, she told her niece, "then I suppose I have to accept, too. Was thinking of asking your father to have a talk with Yohanan, try to dissuade him. Thought maybe my son would listen to him, given his great standing in the Synagogue. But I don't think I shall now. All I shall do is simply inform him of the matter."

"Good, Auntie. This evening we shall take you to him anyway, and to my mother. They will be back by then."

"But only after you have had dinner with us here, of course, everything's ready. My husband and sons will be back at any moment now. It must be getting too dark to work any more.

Elisheva smiled, relieved. "Yes, I would like that very much, thank you."

Maryam went back to peer out of the window, to see whether the men were coming back.

Elisheva's solemn voice came over, "Maryam, listen, after all, our two sons had similar beginnings. We can only expect them to have similar destinies ..."

Maryam turned, was about to reply, but she stopped upon hearing the voices of the men at the door.

YOSEF AND MARYAM

CHAPTER TWENTY SEVEN

"Yosef!"

Yosef ignored the innkeeper's old and wheezy voice. He'd barely heard it over the rowdy din at his usual table, in the corner of the old tavern.

The men sitting there were arguing over the comparative merits of donkeys and mules as multi-purpose beasts of burden. The question was: *if you could afford to own only one, which would you chose?* The argument had heated up, and the several tankards of wine they had consumed had done nothing but fan the flames.

"Yosef!" The innkeeper called out, again to no avail.

Yosef was glowering at Abner the blacksmith, a man built like a rock and possibly the only person in Nazaret who could stand a chance against him should words come to fists. And perhaps that was the reason why Abner persisted in singing the merits of the mule whilst most of his supporters seemed to be shifting sides, confronted by a belligerent Yosef, who repeatedly punctuated his case for the donkey with heavy pounding on the creaking table.

Shimon, who had hitherto watched the scene from a safe distance, his back propped against the counter, finally slunk over.

"Hey Yosef, you break this table and it is I who get paid to fix it, not you, mind you!" He sniggered.

The group of men at the table laughed heartily at this. The argument then resumed once again. Everyone was talking at the same time, but Abner and Yosef were the undisputed champions for each side. Shimon, as usual, sat on the fence, opting to favour whichever side seemed to have the upper hand at that moment. No doubt he was loath to see a final victory for Yosef however, and did not look pleased at the visible increase in his rival's rank of supporters.

"Hey, you guys," he squeaked once more, "know what? I'm tired of hearing the same old arguments over and over again. We're not getting anywhere here. Why don't we settle the matter by casting lots?"

"God himself will decide for us then!" he smirked

Yosef and Abner paused at this, and looking directly into each other's eyes, realised that neither one was going to give way. Shimon pounced on their silence, and taking it as tacit assent, ordered, "Stand up, you two! Prepare your positions. On the count of three now!"

Abner and Yosef stood up and faced each other. All the others gathered round and formed a circle around them. Shimon counted: "one, two ..." then hesitated before the final *'three!'* which he accentuated with a bang of his long-since empty tankard on the table.

Yosef and Abner, who had by the count of two, raised their clenched right fists above their head, now brought these down simultaneously with some fingers exposed, shouting out their predicted sum of the total number of exposed fingers at the same time.

Essentially each man tried to guess how many fingers his opponent would hold out, and then decided how many of his to display, in order to make up the total he would declare.

"Five!" uttered Abner, simultaneously with Yosef's, "Four!" None of the two men won, since Abner had held out two fingers and Yosef only one, thus totalling three. They closed their fists again and raised their right arms to bring them down simultaneously once more, each one again opening his set of fingers.

"Eight!" shouted Abner and "Six!" yelled Yosef—a win for Abner who smirked at the sight of the four fingers opened by Yosef, to be added to his own four. He promptly extended a finger out of his left fist, which served to keep his score. Whoever scored five first would win.

The two men stood rigidly facing each other, each with his score-keeping left arm hanging down and with the right raised high over his head in preparation for its imminent, dramatic, opening drop.

At some unspoken mutual impulse, down came the brawny right arms, splaying fingers as they fell. This time Yosef won with a total of seven against Abner's six: he had three fingers out and the other had four. He flicked a left finger open, almost in Abner's face. The next win was again Abner's, and at this two to one score, Yosef's face whitened in anger.

He thought rapidly but had no time drop his arm and try to get even, for he felt a thin but wiry hand shake him roughly at the shoulder. He spun round angrily. It was the old innkeeper, who yelled up into his face, "Yosef! Have you gone deaf or what? Someone wants to speak with you!"

"So what!" Yosef yelled back down at him, "can't you see I'm in the middle of something? Leave me alone!" He shook his shoulder free and twisted back to face Abner who, with a smirk, was waggling at his face the two left fingers that marked his lead.

The innkeeper, however, grabbed at his shoulder again and shook him even harder. Yosef gritted his teeth, through which he then growled, "Alright, go and ask him to come over then!"

"That is not possible!" stated the innkeeper flatly.

"Why?" Yosef asked, surprised, "is it a woman?"

"No!"

"Is it a Samaritan?"

"No!"

"Come on Yosef, let's continue!" one of the men urged.

But Yosef ignored him, "a Philistine then?"

"No!"

"A Roman?"

"No!"

"A tax collector?"

"No!"

Yosef was evidently listing by increasing nefariousness the *personae non gratae* at the inn.

He had half a mind to ask finally whether it was the Devil himself then, but instead gave up and demanded, "dammit, then *you* tell *me*, who is it?"

The innkeeper rose on his tiptoes and pulling him down to his height whispered the reply into his ear.

Yosef's face darkened, and after a moment, with a defiant glare at his grinning opponent, he lowered his still upraised arm to reach out instead for his tankard. A hush fell.

After taking a deep swig, he started for the door, noting as he went the rest of the men exchanging glances. One or two of them even dared to jeer. Yosef grabbed his leather cape from the peg by the door, and slung it over his broad shoulders.

Not a soul could be seen outside. Not that he was surprised, for the driving rain had not stopped for over three days now. This much rain was unheard of in Nazaret.

It took a few moments for his eyes to adjust to the dim light. Then, through the sheeting rain, he could just make out a figure huddled in a doorway of an abandoned house at some distance to his left. He caught his breath as he recognised him.

It was Azaryahu, from the Leper community.

Yosef flicked on the hood of his cape and started to walk towards him. Then he stopped, thinking it probably wiser to keep his distance.

Azaryahu's strong voice boomed over the pounding rain.

"Yosef, we need you urgently. You must come right away!"

"What?" Yosef shouted. "Come where?"

"To Gadara!"

"What for? In this rain? Any urgent repairs to your tools can wait till tomorrow." He then looked up at the sky, and added, "Provided the rain stops that is, of course. If it will ever stop ..."

Azaryahu made a face, "it is not repairs, Yosef."

"A rake, or a cart then?" Yosef asked, getting somewhat curious now at the reason behind all this urgency. *Surely Azaryahu would not come over in this weather just to order supplies?*

"No, far more urgent! We are in grave danger. We have a disaster over there. This deluge has washed away the foundations of many of our shacks. Three or four have already collapsed with the flood-waters and slid down the hill. Several people have been killed, and many more injured; children, also."

"Well, what do you want from me?"

Azaryahu did not reply but just stood there.

Yosef took a further step towards him and his eyes narrowed. He wasn't sure whether the water streaming down that rugged red face he was looking at was only rain. "Listen, my friend, you can't possibly expect me to enter the Leper area to shore up the shacks?" he asked.

Azaryahu flinched.

"Or do you? Are you mad?"

Azaryahu still did not reply.

"Your people should just get out in the open. Wait till it is all over!"

Azaryahu finally spoke up.

"Yosef, many have done as you say; those that were able to, that is. They are all out there, in a clearing under the foothill, camped out for hours now. But many others are bedridden, or too weak to make it down the hillside: mothers with children too. It is very slippery and dangerous with the mud and all. And God only knows how many more would die if they stayed outside because of the exposure. These are very sick people we are talking about Yosef. They have to remain inside. They have no choice!"

"I can do nothing for you now!" Yosef said firmly, "however, I will come over tomorrow, at dawn, you have my word ... *even* if it's still raining!"

Azaryahu gave him a look of despair.

"Listen, or else I can lend you my tools, would that be alright? "Everything you may need ... tonight. I'd also prepare some struts for you to shore a few houses up. Then you can all just huddle in there. What d'you think? I'll do it, if you just give me a moment to finish up back there," Yosef jerked a huge thumb over his shoulder at the still open doorway of the inn. "That is all I can do tonight. I shall not be long."

He turned to leave, and took a couple of paces towards the inn. Yet he felt Azaryahu's eyes burning into his back. He took a further tentative step, then stopped. With a heavy sigh, he spun round and strode back to the dark figure in the doorway.

"What do you expect of me, exactly?" he asked him. This time his tone was gentler.

"Yosef, listen to me. Please. Of course we do not expect you to enter the settlement. Stay at the post that marks the safe distance. Just prepare the struts, lend us your tools, but please be over there to direct us how and where to set them. That is all. We *need* your directions, you shout them over to us, or if necessary, I will go back and forth each time to convey them to the others, you see? There are several of us who are strong enough for the actual work. They will all help, even some of the women if need be!"

"Tomorrow then?" Yosef tried hopefully.

"*Tonight*, now, Yosef, please, if you can," Azaryahu asked desperately, "tomorrow it may be too late!"

"But it will soon be dusk already!" Yosef pointed out, "how can we work?"

"True, but there is a full moon tonight, Yosef," countered Azaryahu, "you see, not everything is against us at least!"

Yosef looked up. He could not see the moon because of the clouds, but they did look much brighter than they should at this time of the evening.

He heaved a deep sigh.

"Alright, I'm coming, let me finish my wine. I think I am going to need it!" he said with a wan smile. "Go and wait for me outside my house, not too close though, and make sure you are not recognised. We shall then depart together."

As Yosef turned back to the inn, he caught a faint glimpse of someone quickly disappearing from the doorway: *Was that Shimon?* He could not be sure.

The group of men had taken a seat again. They all looked up enquiringly as he strode back to their table, rain-water streaming off his cape.

He did not bother to sit down or confront Abner, or give any sort of explanation.

"The argument is over," he declared. "I lose!"

The others gaped at him as he tilted his head and drained the dregs. Banging the tankard on the table he strode over to the innkeeper, paid his bill and bade him not to tell anyone of his visitor. The old innkeeper nodded wisely; he had been keeping secrets all his life.

CHAPTER TWENTY EIGHT

"Where are you going Papa?" Yosef asked, intrigued, as he watched his father hastily loading the donkey with tools, poles and other lengths of wood.

"Some repairs," Yosef muttered gruffly to his namesake.

"At this hour?" his son asked in a disbelieving tone.

"It cannot wait ... it's this rain, it doesn't look like it is going to stop! Ever! So might as well go now."

"I'll come with you, then."

"No!" Yosef shouted, and his son jumped.

Yosef patted the young man on the shoulder. "Sorry!" he told him. "I didn't mean to shout, it's just that I'm in a hurry and you are distracting me."

"But Papa, why shouldn't I come with you? We shall do the job faster, if there's two of us! We could even get Yaakov and Yehudah maybe. Let me call them."

"I simply don't need you!" Yosef said, raising his voice again, "or any of your brothers. You stay here!"

He then pointed to a stack of logs that were leaning in one corner. "Saw up those logs over there, if you want to work some more; till I return that is."

His son looked puzzled; it was very rare indeed that his father did not take anyone along with him for work.

"Where is it? This job you have to do?" he asked, eyes narrowing, "here in Nazaret?"

His father's voice rose again.

"Will you just stop asking questions and let me get on with it?"

The young man did stop at this. Yosef could just see his son's mind racing, probably thinking, *'Maybe it is some work for the Romans, and Papa is too ashamed to let anyone know.'* They had recently discussed whether it would be all right for them to finally accept work from the hated occupier of their land. The family was indeed large: five boys and three girls, several with husbands and wives and their own children. And although their trade was in demand and the fields rendered a good crop, they needed every extra penny they could get. Working for the invader was widely looked down upon, true, but it wasn't the deadliest of sins.

The door opened and Yaakov stepped in, followed by his younger brothers, Shimon and Yehudah. "Hey Papa, there's Azaryahu down at the corner!" He shouted excitedly.

The son who'd been named for him gave Yosef an understanding look, then raised his eyebrows questioningly. Blushing, his father affirmed it with a nod.

"Papa," Yosef asked gently, "are you sure about this? Is it really necessary?

His father grunted and continued loading the donkey.

"I'll come and help you, anyway," Yosef continued.

"So will I," Yaakov said solemnly, noticing the laden donkey and realizing the purpose of Azaryahu's presence.

Yehudah, with his blank face, showed he understood nothing, but all the same said, "me too!"

"And me!" shouted little Shimon, the youngest of the brothers, clearly understanding even less, "we'll all go with you!"

Yosef looked up, gave too strong a tug at the harness strap and the donkey brayed. He quickly loosened the strap again a little, and spun round to face his four sons, a rebuke at the ready on his lips for their insistence. Yet this never left them for he suddenly noticed Yeshua at the corner of the workshop. *Just standing there, silently looking on, like some ghost.*

None of them could ever get quite used to the disconcerting fact that Yeshua seemed to appear and disappear in places without anyone noticing. It was as if his feet never really touched the ground, and thus he could not be heard coming—and as if his form faded, and could not be seen.

"So shall I," Yeshua now said, softly.

"None of you are coming!" Yosef replied through his teeth. "How many times do I have to say it? You stay right here, all of you. Don't get me angry now!"

He looked over to the heavily laden donkey, checking whether he had packed all he would need. He pursed his lips. He felt sure he had forgotten something, but he could not place exactly what. This argument with his sons had distracted him. Finally, he gave a shrug, and then a nod, and looked at them. They were standing there in a silent group, giving him worried looks.

"Come on!" he told them with a laugh. He stepped over and hugged each one in turn. "It is not as if I am going to my death, you know!"

He pulled his namesake to him and, wrapping a burly arm around his shoulders, prepared to whisper in his ear. He did not have to stoop in doing this, and felt the usual buck at the fact that his son had reached his height. "They need some urgent work done, my son," he told him. "It is a matter of life and death, you see. I have to go, but I'll be careful, I promise."

He then stepped to the door, opened it and, grasping the reins, led his donkey out. As it swayed, the two brightly lit lanterns swung back and forth from the saddle and threw crazy shadows onto the dusky alley. Raindrops that caught the light flashed it back like tiny darts. At the corner he met the silently waiting Azaryahu. Yosef glanced back over his shoulder to see his five boys gazing solemnly at him from the lit doorway. He waved goodbye to them and they, somewhat hesitantly, waved back.

YOSEF AND MARYAM

CHAPTER TWENTY NINE

The road to Gadara seemed endless.

Yosef had been on it more than once before, yet this time it seemed to have no end to it.

Perhaps it was because of the fierce gusts of wind that was making them sway on the road. Or perhaps because the donkey kept slipping on the streaming mud they had to trudge through in several places.

No, that's not it! Yosef said to himself. It must be because he wanted the job over and done with, quickly, so he'd be able to go back to his sons and reassure them.

But no! No, not even that was quite the reason. What was it then?

It then dawned on him: *Azaryahu.*

The old man was striding through the rain with a resolute drive, spurred with an urgency Yosef had never ever seen before, on anyone. And he must have passed this onto him.

That's it!

He realised just how much the community depended on this one man: their only link with the outside world. Azaryahu gathered alms for the Lepers, sanitised their handiwork for sale, brought them supplies. He managed to keep them just a short distance away from the precipice of complete isolation, and the annihilation that that would bring. This he managed by keeping his own distance from them, living on his own, without a family, halfway between Gadara and Nazaret.

This man is not doing it out of some aspiration to sanctitude, even though he has no relatives among them, and so is not bound to help them in any way. He does it because he genuinely loves them; loves the disfigured, bedraggled Lepers!

Yosef shook his head again and again in wonder. *Maybe his wasn't the biggest heart to claim in the land after all.*

The mountain and hills of Gadara finally loomed into view. Black mounds against an eerily lit sky. And with some difficulty, through the sheeting rain, one could even at times make out the darker silhouettes of the rickety shacks that criss-crossed the hill-face.

'Like some crazy out-of-control vine, Yosef thought, *'These Lepers have done well for themselves, for the strands of this "vine" sprawl all over the place ...'*

It was clear that Azaryahu had certainly succeeded in his mission, and that there was little chance that the community would ever die off, as many people in Nazaret hoped, not altogether secretly.

Yosef paused at the point of the road which, long ago, someone had established as being the minimum distance safe against infection, from the closest shacks of the settlement. The rickety board flashed out its inscribed dire warning in Latin and Hebrew as the pole it was hammered to, bent and swayed back and forth in the gusting wind. And the ancient discoloured skull that crowned it served as the most graphic of warnings to those who could not read.

The two men looked grimly at the hillside. Most of the rows of shacks still seemed intact; swaying but still clinging to the rocky slope as heavy rain poured on them, and as muddy torrents streamed all around them. The wind was making some of the shutters bang in rapid rhythms, as if forcing their base accompaniment to its high-pitched wail. *'A mad cacophony, indeed,'* Yosef thought.

He looked to his left at a large group of people huddled together in a field. They looked grey and black, and thoroughly soaked like some massive horde of huge rats. And there were hundreds of them. The hair on the back of his neck stood up and he gave a shudder. The crowd was mostly silent though.

Then, a woman wailed, and would not be silenced: "My daughter, my daughter ...!" she shrieked, standing up and pointing with a quivering bandaged hand towards the shacks. Yosef could just make out the words.

Azaryahu had told him that some people could not get out of their houses, and he looked up and down in dismay at the rows, wondering how he could tell in which of these they were sheltering.

Despite the rain, the visibility was amazing. The full moon beamed its cold light down fiercely through gaps in the scudding clouds. It made the rain-drops glint like arrowheads, and it threw harsh shadows that accentuated the ugliness of the scene, in stark black and white. *Uglier in its light, true*, yet Yosef knew that without this radiance his task would be hopeless. *Still, it was going to take all night.*

Azaryahu had already organised a gang of about a dozen or so of the most able-bodied men. They quickly set about carrying the poles and tools over to the hillside. Yosef had surveyed the scene intensely and picked out the weakest point so they could shore that up first. From the post, he barked his orders to Azaryahu who in turn ran and relayed them back to the men.

The going was slow, and it wasn't going to be easy. Yosef knew that most of the men had missing thumbs or fingers, and nearly all were limping. The large pole they had managed to jam at an angle against the bottom shack had already slipped a couple of times.

They finally managed to lever a huge boulder to its foot, and it thankfully held. The men then shuffled over to the other side of the row and started doing the same thing to a tottering old shack that was swaying very badly in the gusting wind.

They were making progress but the pace was too slow.

If only these people weren't infectious and my sons were with me. Yosef dismally surveyed the heavy clouds to the west, and realised there would be no let-up of the storm any time soon.

He then snapped his head back down and around as a jarring crash was heard. A wail rose up from the crowd.

The shack the work-gang had first shored up had suddenly collapsed, and the foundations it displaced as it slewed downhill had brought the two adjacent shacks down with it.

Bodies could be seen in the rolling debris, arms and legs tangling madly with blankets, clothing and pieces of wood. Two men, who had been running towards him to get struts from the post, halted and looked back in shock. They paused for only a moment though. The horrific scene spurred them into frenzied action and they doubled their hobbling pace. Yosef bit his lower lip to stifle a curse.

"Here Azaryahu," he shouted over the thundering sound of the rain, "take the donkey. Go on, use it, we're getting nowhere otherwise; it's useless at this rate!" He hurled over the reins.

"But—!" Azaryahu started. Once the donkey came into contact with the Lepers, it could never go back.

"Take it, take it!" Yosef yelled. "There's no time to argue. It's alright, you can buy me another one in due course," he told him, knowing full well that he never could. "Forget that side of the hill. Change of plans! Shore up that big shack in the middle now, quickly!"

Azaryahu nodded and yanked the donkey towards the men. They loaded a huge pole on its back and, leading it up the slippery hillside, arrived at the middle shack. They tried to set the pole up to buttress the side, but it kept slipping.

Yosef shouted over to them to use two smaller poles instead and nail a thwart across them. But the more he shouted, the more the wind seemed to rise in intensity as if to purposely muffle his voice. The workers kept in vain trying to shore up the side of the shack with single poles, which they had fetched over from the back of the still-laden, heavily panting donkey.

Yosef shouted at the top of his voice at Azaryahu, but the old man was engrossed in holding a tall and heavy strut up as the others tugged and pushed at a large roundish boulder they found nearby. They apparently wanted to roll this against the foot of the support. Two of them attempted to lever it clear of the ground with poles, whilst another was frantically digging at the soil under it with a spade.

"Forget that boulder!" Yosef screamed, "it's too big and too round! Come over here, Azaryahu!" But the increased distance from the post prevented Azaryahu from hearing his command. He yelled again and again in vain—the wind just whipped his words away the moment they came out of his mouth.

"Mister!"

The tiny voice came from behind him. Yosef spun round to behold a little boy—bedraggled, half-naked, and utterly soaked. He took a step back with a shudder. The boy had a large red patch on his left cheek: yet his light eyes were alive, bright and piercing, possibly more so because he had no eyelashes and no eyebrows.

"Mister, shall I go get Azaryahu for you? He can't hear you!" he asked plaintively. He was shivering so much that he was shaking the rain off like some dog.

Yosef took a couple of further steps backwards, alarmed at seeing him so close. But then he gave him a nod. The boy spun on his heels to run quickly towards the hill, and then up to the shacks.

The workers had by this time dislodged the boulder. They were trying to position it against the foot of the strut when one of the men slipped and reached out for it for balance. He managed to grab it, then gave a scream when, as if with a life of its own, it rolled towards him. He stumbled and fell back, and the boulder rolled right over his legs crushing them. With another terrible scream, the man flailed the ground with his arms, and convulsed crazily, while the boulder continued rolling and gaining momentum down the hillside.

The others all stopped what they were doing and rushed over to his aid.

All but two of them who instead ran beside the heavily trundling boulder and threw sticks and rocks in front of it. Their attempts at stopping it were futile. It continued on its relentless rampage and smashed right through a shack, and then through another, its speed barely diminishing. Azaryahu was watching its destructive path in alarm when he spied with a start a little boy running up the hill towards them. He was running so fast that he had his head down. Azaryahu sped down the hill waving his arms wildly and screaming at him to get out of the way.

The boy heard him and, looking up, stopped dead in his tracks at the sight of the huge boulder trundling heavily and directly towards him. Although he had plenty of time to jump clear, he simply could not move. He was rooted to the spot in terror. His eyes looked up its face as it rose in front of him. The boy was crushed like a rag-doll. The men at the hillside gave a wail; several fell down to their knees and beat their faces in despair.

The large rock then bounded and splashed down the rest of the hillside, just missing the group in the open field by a narrow margin. It finally rolled slowly to a halt in the plain.

The lepers looked at its cold hard mass, dark and streaked with mud and blood.

Azaryahu looked at the broken body of the boy at his feet. The head was the only part of the tiny body that had escaped being crushed, and that look of surprise was still imprinted on his tiny face: eyes looking up blankly at the sky. He followed his gaze and stared questioningly at the vast domed expanse it pointed to.

The moon, right above, its face fat and greedy in its fullness, looked back down at him, appearing through the rain from behind the dark cloud where it had been hiding.

It was all-seeing, yet silent, unfeeling.

Yosef stood dazed and transfixed as he witnessed the mounting disaster. Heart pounding, he tottered in helpless agitation. The Lepers in the field were wailing and now huddling even closer to each other.

They weren't safe even out there in the plain!

The men on the hillside had slumped to the ground and lost all their will to continue. The one with crushed legs had also fallen silent.

A huge jarring squeak then came over from the shacks. The middle one they had been trying to shore up gave a judder, and part of its roof fell in.

Yosef gave a grunt and grabbed at the sack that contained his lime bucket. He stared into it in disbelief. There was no lime in there, just metal clasps and wooden wedges. *Nothing to protect myself with!* With a cry of anger, he flung it to the ground.

Yosef gritted his teeth, gave a bound and sped towards the shacks.

As he reached them, the men scrambled up, amazed.

"Come on!" he urged, "have you given up or what? Here, you! *Yes, you!* Fetch me that long pole, and you, those two short ones over there, quickly now!"

Azaryahu stood there staring at him, the look on his face almost comically shifting from relief to dismay and back again.

He was trembling.

Yosef stepped over to him, and gave him a resounding slap on his shoulder, "don't worry, my friend, the heavy rain will cleanse me! Or maybe I get to find out that I'm like you, immune!" He then turned back to the men. They had not moved.

"Didn't you hear what I just said?" he yelled at them.

They paused for just one more moment, and then quickly did as directed. Yosef placed a strut athwart the two short poles, and kneeling, grabbed the hammer. As he frantically searched the ground around him for the nail sack, he felt a prod at his back. Twisting round, he saw a withered hand with just two fingers handing down a huge nail. He looked up to see the toothless, grinning face of a young man. *He had no nose.* Yosef took the nail from him gingerly, then quickly hammered it into the wood.

The support was constructed in no time at all, and the men enthusiastically helped Yosef wedge it into place. As the shack shook with a fresh gust of wind, it shuddered for a moment, then seemed to hold. Yosef quickly nailed a supporting plank into the ground at its foot.

Satisfied, he stepped back and climbed uphill to look for the next point to shore up. He stepped close to a window whose last remaining shutter was flailing uselessly against the wall. Peering inside he saw a woman on the floor, in the corner, huddled up in wet blankets. She held a baby in her arms. Through a large gap in the ceiling, silver banks of clouds could be seen moving across the sky.

The woman looked over at him, terrified. Her face was young and looked perfectly normal, but her swollen and purplish leg could be seen jutting out from under a blanket. The foot was just a blunt knob wrapped in a piece of cloth.

Yosef gave her a wide smile and she ventured an uncertain smile back at him. In some strange way she reminded him of the adulteress he had put out of her misery, many years before. With a shake of his head, he turned to the men who were still gazing contentedly at the steady strut.

"Come on men!" he shouted, almost gleefully, "back to work now, we haven't even started yet!"

Azaryahu broke into a run and caught up with the others who, led by Yosef, were making their way towards a creaking shack further uphill.

After its support was hammered in place, Yosef suddenly realised they had used up the last of the poles. He sped down to one of the collapsed shacks. Most of the wood strewn about seemed shattered and useless. But he finally spied a suitable pole in the debris. A dead woman lay under it. Yosef could not be sure whether the gash on her forehead was an injury or had been caused by her leprosy. Making his way over, he lifted the arm she had across the pole and, laying it gently by her side, heaved the pole onto his shoulder. He turned and looked back at her. She now seemed to be just sleeping.

****

By the time they had finished, a faint yellowish glow to the east could be seen. The storm had still not abated. Yosef kicked at the base of the few shacks still worth saving, and was satisfied that the immediate danger was over. Azaryahu and the men raced downhill to help everyone get back inside.

Giving a heavy sigh, Yosef walked over to his donkey. It had been tethered by someone to a fig tree. He patted it on the neck.

"Goodbye, my friend," he whispered into its large, twitching ear, patting it on the neck. Then, thinking for a moment he grimly added, "Or maybe I should say, till we meet again!"

The men followed him and thanked him profusely as he trudged his way back to the post. Then they all stopped. Azaryahu stood and stared at his receding back—drilling his eyes into him.

Yosef had almost reached the circle of small stones that surrounded the gruesome pole when he stopped in his tracks. There were people standing there. Five silhouettes materialised against the western sky, — still too dark to make out who they were, though: five men. They were just standing there, looking over at him.

Yosef walked on and stopped a short distance away from his sons.

Yaakov heaved and hurled something over. It landed with a heavy thud at Yosef's feet.

The sack of lime.

"You forgot this!" he said to him, his voice choked in anger. He then spun swiftly on his heels and strode away.

His brother Yosef gave his father a look of despair, and with a half-stifled sob, hung his head down low and turned back too, tugging the silently weeping Shimon and Yehudah away with him.

Yosef took a couple of steps towards them, and halted as he found himself facing Yeshua, who had not moved.

Yeshua's own face was calm and sedate, appearing as if lit from within. His unwavering gaze at Yosef's face was placid and understanding. And it radiated more love than Yosef had seen in anyone's eyes—*ever.*

'Those eyes...' he wondered, yet again, as he had for countless times. He looked dizzily into them, wishing to dive in and float away in their waters.

YOSEF AND MARYAM

CHAPTER THIRTY

Yosef gave a grunt and rolled over for the umpteenth time that night. The tent he'd erected wasn't big and once again, his foot had banged on the pole at the far end, knocking it over. It had collapsed almost entirely on top of him and as he sat up, his head pushed against its roof.

"Damn board!" he hissed. The clickety-clack of wood against wood came across from the windswept board yet again, in defiant reply.

'They should get some carpenter to fix it!' he thought, grinning at his own joke. He yawned, then crawled out on all fours. While still on his knees, Yosef blinked in the sunlight, and rummaging in a sack, fished out a hammer and some nails. He upended a bucket next to the sign-post and stepping carefully onto it, was just able to reach up and hammer a couple of nails into the board. The gusty morning wind tugged at his stringy hair and clotted beard and seemed intent on toppling him off his perch. He gave it a tug and, satisfied, hopped off. He threw the hammer and remaining nails into the sack and gave his habitual look at the invariably empty road to Nazaret.

Yosef started in surprise as he saw a wagon approaching this time. *Is it his sons again?* He squinted. *Is that the Carpenter's wagon? Shimon's? Could it be possible? Yes it is! That's him, and he has a passenger.*

The wagon stopped a good distance away and the passenger alighted with a bound. A woman.

Yosef dropped his hammer as he recognised Maryam immediately.

"Yosef!" she shouted, breaking into a run.

"You stop there, Maryam, right there I say!" Yosef yelled, jabbing his finger at her. His voice was thunderous and served to stop her dead in her tracks.

"But Yosef!" she sobbed.

"Do not move a single step closer!" he called out, "it's not safe, not safe at all."

He had been camped out for over a week now, right outside the stone circle that surrounded the post, waiting for something to happen. The day after the storm, his sons had brought over a tent, as well as plenty of food and a barrel of water. He had informed Yeshua earlier on that it was not safe for him to go back into the village until he was absolutely sure he had not been infected.

His sons, although heartbroken at Yeshua's words, had reluctantly agreed with their father, and swiftly loaded his requirements onto the wagon.

Every morning since then, he had stripped stark naked and upturned a bucket of lime-wash all over him, letting it dry in the sun, and then rinsing himself thoroughly.

Once some of it had gotten into his eyes and he had screamed out in pain. After this incident, he wasn't at all sure his eyesight had come completely back to normal, and he fervently hoped this was only because of the caustic lime. *But he wasn't sure—not sure at all.*

"Yosef, our children did not tell me about this ... this madness! They *lied* to me!" Maryam screamed at him, shaking her head in disbelief. "They said you'd gone to Yerushalayim!"

Yosef limped back a couple of paces. Maryam wailed and started forward again, screaming, "Yosef are you alright? What happened to your leg? When are you coming home? Are you clean?" She lunged forward.

"Stop right there!" Yosef yelled once more, but this time Maryam gave no heed. In a fit of anger, he grabbed a rock and hurled it to the ground in front of her. It shattered and a fragment struck her.

It was only a slight pinch, yet she gave a squeal of surprise and with a look of consternation stopped in her tracks.

"Stop, I tell you!" he warned her. "I'm not letting you *anywhere* near me, even if I have to maim you to do it!"

Maryam collapsed into a heap and started crying, beating at the ground with her fist, "why ... why did you do it, Yosef?" She shook her head in disbelief, barely mouthing the words, "tell me you are clean. Come back home now with me! I will take care of you."

"I cannot!" he replied wistfully, wishing very hard he *could* tell her he was clean.

But he had seen the knowing glances the Lepers were giving him, although they said nothing and still kept their distance. Azaryahu also could not look him in the eye, and seemed to be avoiding him.

And he knew his knee had swelled up all of a sudden, without his having injured it, at least as far as he could remember. His heart had also been recently hammering for no reason at all during the night, and he feared the worst—and after all was said and done, the inevitable.

"Maryam, listen to me, please. I had to come over here and save them," he said in a voice that, albeit hoarse, was so calm and steady that he himself was surprised. "You know how I am. More than anyone. At the village they always said that my heart was bigger than my head. So, it got the better of me once and for all, I suppose."

He stiffened as he had a flashback of Maryam weeping when she came over to tell him she was with child—a child that was not his. And how in his kindness, he had resolved to send her away quietly.

His eyes misted over: again he was now sending her away.

Maryam gazed at him now, stunned. She rocked back and forth on the stony ground in despair.

So he threw her a loving look, one he hoped she could see at that distance. But Maryam had already pulled her shawl over her head and was sobbing heavily into it.

Yosef lifted his eyes off her and noticed Shimon for the first time, who cautiously blinked at him from beside the wagon, where he was nervously pacing back and forth.

As he saw Yosef glowering in his direction, he called out to him defensively, "Yosef, listen, I had to bring her over! Your sons refused to!"

Yosef nodded, "it's alright Shimon. Take her back now! Maybe I'm clean, maybe I'm not. If I don't make it, please, try to help out my sons if you can, at least with advice on the work and things, I mean."

Shimon nodded vigorously and in a weak voice, summoned Maryam over.

She shook her head vehemently and then raised it to look at Yosef.

"Go on, Maryam," Yosef encouraged her, his voice still strong and calm. "There's nothing you can do for me here. Go back to Nazaret! Maybe I can come back home soon, who knows? We just have to pray."

"No!" Maryam screamed, "this is wrong! This cannot be; this is not right!"

She struggled to her feet and started forward again.

"Shimon!" Yosef yelled over alarmed.

And Shimon, sensing his bidding, bounded towards Maryam and started tugging her back. Screaming, she lashed out and, being taller and heavier, overpowered him and broke free.

"Maryam!" Yosef screamed furiously at her. He raised one hand towards her and swung the other in the direction of the shacks, "you take one more step forward and I will run right back there into those Lepers' houses!

"I mean it, woman!" he threatened, "then I'll catch the disease for sure. I'm warning you! *I'll do it!*"

Maryam stopped, dropping her arms helplessly to her side. She could always tell when Yosef really meant it. Defeated, she could hardly lift her eyes off the ground.

His voice came over, gasping his relief, "go back and take care of our children. Don't worry about me. You have to obey me! It is your duty!"

Maryam shook and trembled as Shimon delicately pulled her back to the wagon.

As they sat next to each other he gently picked off a tiny shard of rock which was stuck to her woollen shawl, looked at it, and then tossed it away.

He wiped the sweat off his brow, gave a sudden sneeze and a sigh, then wheeled the mule round and back towards Nazaret.

Maryam looked back at her husband over her shoulder.

He was standing gauntly next to a pole with a skull on it, looking back at them with intensity. He already looked thinner—much thinner.

She gave a shudder, as she saw him almost resembling that deathly pole he was holding on to. He waved to them as they approached the turn in the road that would hide them from view and she raised her own hand feebly in response.

YOSEF AND MARYAM

CHAPTER THIRTY ONE

On the seemingly endless road back, Maryam's thoughts drifted back to the events of the last few hours.

She had rushed to Shimon's house, which lay in its own grounds in the middle of the village. Marta, his wife, was not there, and the housekeeper had openly leered at her as she let her in. With a huff, she had gone to inform her master that someone was asking for him.

Shimon had come in to greet her from his workshop. Hastily putting aside his apron, he had nervously brushed specks of sawdust from his sparse and oily hair.

"Why, Maryam, what brings you here? How are you?" he asked, seeming much surprised at her visit, "Marta is not here ..."

"It is you I wanted to see," Maryam interrupted him. She gave a sidelong glance at the housekeeper. Shimon got the message immediately, and bade his servant to leave them alone. This the woman did hesitantly. With an even greater huff, she finally stepped outside the room and reluctantly closed the door behind her.

After the exchange of some pleasantries, Shimon winked at Maryam and opened the door again.

The housekeeper was just halfway down the corridor, pretending to dust a spotless old oak casket. He scowled at her and with her loudest huff so far, she finally moved out into the courtyard.

"What is it, Maryam?" he asked again, feeling that something was definitely up.

"I need a favour from you, Shimon!" she replied.

Shimon raised his eyebrows, and waited.

"Do you know where my husband is?" Her tone was eager, almost pleading.

"Yosef?" Shimon asked and thought for a moment.

"Isn't he in Yerushalayim?"

"That's what my sons told me!" Maryam said icily. *They lied!"*

Shimon cocked his head to one side. "They all *lied* to you? Even Yeshua?"

"Well, Yeshua said nothing, in his usual way ..."

"So where is he? Yosef, I mean ..." Shimon asked.

"He is in Gadara."

"So?"

"He isn't in the actual city, he's in the hills, near the Lepers' settlement!" Maryam whimpered.

Shimon sneered. "That fool, that utter fool!" he spat out without any attempt to hide the contempt he felt, "are you certain? How did you get to find out then?"

"Well, I didn't feel right about this sudden '*Yerushalayim*' job. He always informs me about these trips before leaving. This time he just left, in the middle of the night, without even saying goodbye. I sensed something was wrong from the start. Days passed, almost a week, and he failed to turn up. And my sons were whispering all the time, behaving strangely, long faces all round. My daughters knew nothing. Then last night I couldn't sleep and at dawn it finally occurred to me to have a good look at his workshop, and ..."

"And?" Shimon asked.

"His sack of lime was missing!"

Shimon indicated he understood, and gave her a nod.

"So I woke the children up straight away. They continued to deny; so finally I confronted Yeshua, who had to admit.

"My husband has been over there for over a week now!" Maryam gave a sob.

"What? He has been over there for a whole week?" Shimon sounded incredulous. Then his brow furrowed and darkened.

196

"See, Maryam, do you see now what a fool he is and what a bigger fool *you* were to marry him?" he asked her angrily.

Maryam glared at him through her tears and he glared back at her. After a moment he swiftly spun round, picked something up from on top of a rosewood cabinet, and handed it over.

She hesitantly took it in her hands. It was an inlaid jewellery box, one she had seen before. It was chipped on one side, and she ran a delicate finger over the groove.

"It chipped when I tried to fix the hinge. That is why I did not give it back to you, at that time," he told her sullenly.

Maryam gave him a knowing look, showing him she knew that wasn't the real reason.

"Yes, Maryam, it is chipped ... like my heart. Open it!"

"Why should I?" she protested, "it's not mine, it is Marta's."

"It *could* have been yours!" Shimon cried. "Go on, open it I say!"

Maryam tentatively lifted the clasp open. '*It isn't so hard now,*' she thought. Her eyes lit up at the gold and silver jewellery that glittered back at her. She stood transfixed looking at the contents for a while. Then, she fingered a beautiful gold necklace inlaid with emeralds. Ever so slowly, and hardly aware of what she was doing, she delicately lifted it, placed it to her neck and looked at herself in the small mirror that was set inside the lid.

"The colour of the stones matches Marta's eyes perfectly," Shimon stated gravely.

Maryam jumped and dropped the necklace back inside the box, promptly slamming the lid shut with a bang.

"Want to break it again?" Shimon asked her in stark sarcasm.

"Shimon," Maryam replied weakly, "listen, I can well understand your bitterness, but it just was not meant for the two of us to be together, that is all. Marta is indeed beautiful, more than I am, I'm sure. And she has given you a son. What more do you want? Why aren't you happy?"

"Who said I wasn't happy?" Shimon, enraged, screamed at her. He calmed down after a while and went on, "yes, she is beautiful, a good mother and housekeeper too. And ..."

"She is also faithful ...," he added whilst looking pointedly at Maryam with a dark, shrewd eye.

Maryam's eyes blazed her response back at him.

She thrust the box back into his hands.

"Maryam, I just wanted to be happier, that is all, and to have made you happier.

"Look at you now!" he said with a sneer.

Maryam winced, yet her response was enounced softly.

"Love is never a choice. If it were, it wouldn't be true love at all."

Shimon froze at these words.

Shaking his head, he then stepped reluctantly to the cabinet to place the jewellery box back on top of it. He looked over his shoulder at her, "so what do you want from me, what have you come here for?"

"I want you to take me to him. It's a long way off, I cannot go by myself."

"What?" he turned to face her. "Are you crazy? I am not going anywhere *near* that place. I have never had anything to do with those people. *Ever*! God forbid! It isn't worth it!"

Maryam looked at him, her eyes pleading; her palms open at her sides.

"Ask your sons to take you!" he responded with a shrug.

"They refuse to take me there! Shimon, I cannot trust anyone else. I don't want people to know. People can be cruel, they would not come anywhere near us, we'd starve."

"And yet you trust me, and expect this of me? This grave risk to my health? To my life even! No way!"

"Shimon, if ever you truly loved me, you would do this for me!"

"No!" Shimon rapped on the cabinet with the box, and Maryam jumped. "Yosef was my rival in everything. He won, almost always. Why should I care about him? *No!*"

"No? You won't take me ...? But what about me? Don't you care for me? Did you really ever love me?"

Shimon gritted his teeth. "No, what I meant was ... I mean I would only do this for you, not for him ... if I *still* loved you."

Maryam's eyes looked directly into his, and misted over.

His eyes, always red-brimmed, turned redder still.

After what seemed like an eternity, he gave a sigh. "Let me saddle the mule," he conceded in a choked voice, his head hung low.

A whinnying bray from the mule, probably as it caught sight of the village, brought Maryam back to the present, and the road back home. She saw that they were by now quite close to Nazaret and dusk had fallen. Feeling very cold, she glanced over at Shimon. He slouched over the reins, also deeply lost in thought.

"Shimon ..." she whispered.

He did not respond and soon, as they had agreed, dropped her off at the outskirts of the village. There was no one was in sight. Before she left, she thanked him and asked him to promise her again that he would not tell anyone, not even Marta, about Yosef.

Shimon grunted, but gave her a nod.

Maryam pulled her shawl close to her cheeks against the cold, and tried to find his eyes. But he looked aside and with a slap of the reins, quickly spurred the mule on, down the road.

YOSEF AND MARYAM

CHAPTER THIRTY TWO

"Yosef!" Azaryahu repeated for the third time. He dodged as a spadeful of earth flew over his head, just missing him. With a sigh he gave up trying to get Yosef's attention by voice alone.

He peered down the huge hole that the big man was busy digging out, on his own, shovelling out and throwing spadefuls of soil and rubble over his broad shoulders. Soon they would have a new well and God only knew how much they needed it. But heretofore, no one had the faintest idea of how to go about the task.

Yosef had been a Godsend to the community. Practically everyone's life had changed for the better over the few weeks since he had joined their ranks. It had taken less than two weeks for the signs of leprosy to become unmistakable on Yosef's face and body, at which he had resolutely moved over from the post and pitched his tent next to the shacks.

There was no going back now. He had immediately set about constructing a small shack for himself out of the debris from the storm, and ever since, had never stopped working on the requirements of the community.

Azaryahu picked up a pebble and tossed it at Yosef, hitting him squarely in the back. Yosef ignored it, if he felt it at all. Azaryahu frowned, then threw a larger stone at the same moment that Yosef straightened up to wipe his brow.

It hit him on the top of his large head.

He cried out in pain, and a small jet of crimson blood gushed out. Yosef rubbed his head, gazed at the blood on his palm, and looked up to see an embarrassed Azaryahu peering down into the hole, right next to the head of his donkey. Azaryahu looked devastated, but the donkey appeared to be grinning down at him.

"Hey, sorry! I'm so sorry," Azaryahu whined.

"Hey, was that you?" Yosef shouted up in mock anger. "Why in heaven's name do you want to kill me? Is this your way of thanking me for all the work I've been doing for you? For free?

"Could you not at least wait till the well is finished? Or am I digging my own grave here?"

He rubbed his big head again but his widening grin then gave him away.

"Sorry, sorry!" Azaryahu, now befuddled, kept repeating all the same, "I just wanted to attract your attention, you see, you cannot ..." He could not quite bring himself to say the word.

"*Hear*," Yosef finished his sentence for him. The leprosy had affected his hearing very badly and everyone now had to shout for him to understand. Or otherwise make sure they faced him, as they spoke, for he had quickly been taught to lip-read by the others.

"What is it then?" Yosef asked, his voice louder than necessary.

"There is someone to see you," the old man said, mouthing the words more emphatically than was really necessary.

"At the post?"

"Yes."

Yosef's face turned grim. He climbed up the shaky rough ladder he'd made himself, and hopped out.

"It's a woman," Azaryahu added.

"What's the wind like?" Yosef asked, brushing the dust and soil off his clothes with his calloused hands.

"The wind is fine."

The Lepers would only talk to visitors at the post if they could stand downwind of them, as an extra safeguard against infection. Needless to say, despite all the precautions, visitors to the settlement were very rare indeed.

Giving the last quick brushes to his clothing, he limped over towards the post, stamping the loose soil out of his sandals on his way.

He came to a halt at the circle of small stones marking the safe distance, at a point where the makeshift wind-vane pointed directly at him.

"What are you doing here?" he demanded of the woman at the post.

He saw her lips move, but could just barely hear her reply, even with the aid of the wind. He always felt a grim satisfaction when remembering that this downwind precaution ironically compensated for his loss of hearing.

"You will have to shout!" he informed her, "I am practically deaf now."

"I said, what are *you* doing here?" Was her stony reply.

Yosef looked down at his feet, his face clouding over.

"I have no choice but to be here," he replied, looking up again.

"You are a liar!" Her angry retort was more audible now.

He gave her a confused, pleading look. It had little effect, for her words remained hard.

"You may certainly have no choice now," she went on icily, "but before you had!"

The woman appeared very agitated, and was trembling all over.

"Love is never a choice!" he shouted back.

"You are telling *me!*" she screamed in response.

"You may not be able to choose *whether* to love or not, true," she continued angrily, "but surely you can choose just *how much* to love, can't you? Just for *once* in your life."

Yosef said nothing.

"To love is to lose, Yosef. Don't you see that?"

"Lose?" he asked, confused.

"Yes, lose. *Lose!*" she screamed, "to love you must give, and that which is given, is therefore lost. You only lose nothing if you love only yourself. Because whatever you give, you give to yourself!"

"You loved Maryam, and lost me," Marta went on.

"You loved God and lost your dignity as a husband.

"And as a father, you lost the first-born of your family."

Yosef raised his eyebrows and gave a shudder.

Marta saw it and added sardonically, "oh yes, I do know, Yosef.

"Do you think a woman does not say *everything* to her best friend? Maryam told me about it, a long time ago. So I always knew. And I am not the only one who knows, either."

Yosef hung his head. "I had a dream, Marta ...," he started, his voice barely above a whisper, "Yeshua ..."

"Oh you had a dream, did you?" Marta interrupted him. "Well I had a dream too, Yosef. Where is it now? Mine didn't come true, at all! And what makes you so sure yours was real? Grow up, Yosef. Stop dreaming and wake up to this world, this *cruel* world!"

"I know it was just a dream, Marta, but it was *my* dream, and it was real for me. I want to believe. I have no choice but to believe. And ... I *do* believe."

"Yes, you did, and most probably you still do. Fine. But that was not enough for you, was it?" she rebuked him. "You had to go even further, and love your neighbour too, as yourself!

"Well, *I* was your neighbour! Your real neighbour! Did you love me? *No!* Which neighbours did you choose to love then? Perfect strangers! *Lepers even!*" She clasped her hands to her ears in despair.

"Look at you now!" she screamed at him.

Yosef gritted his teeth. "Have you come to comfort me?" he mocked. "Go back! Go back to your husband. *Go!* Go back to Shimon. You, for one, did not marry him for love, did you? So *you* lost nothing!"

"No, I did not! And neither did he," she hissed through her teeth.

"Then you married each other just to show us, to get back at us! At me and Maryam!"

Marta gave a twisted smile.

"Maybe," she replied coolly, "or maybe we simply had to settle for second best."

"You hate me now, don't you?" he asked in a strangled voice.

"Yes! I hate you because I love you. I hate your choices. I hate what you put yourself through, and consequently, what you put *me* through."

"And so, you came over here to gloat? To prove yourself right?" Yosef regretted the words as soon as they were out of his mouth.

Tears streamed from the woman's face but he could not hear her sobbing.

"I didn't really mean that, sorry!" he hastily shouted over.

"Is that what you really think?" she asked grimly, ignoring his apology.

"Hey, what are you doing?" Yosef yelled, at seeing her taking several quick steps towards him.

"I want to stay with you! Live with you," she said, as she continued forward. "I want to comfort you."

"Are you mad?" Yosef screamed, taking a few steps back himself, "stop! Stay away, woman! I'm telling you!"

"I mean it!" she screamed back. "I don't care about the disease!"

"Stop right there!" he bellowed. "Not one more step forward!"

The sheer force of his command came like a wave to stop her in her tracks.

"What about Yehudah, your only son?!" Yosef shouted over. "Marta! Do you want to betray him as you accuse me of doing to those whom I love? Are you ready to abandon him?"

"Well, Yehudah abandoned me," Marta replied flatly. "As you know, he has been living in Kerios for over three years now. We seldom see his face. They even call him now *Yehudah the Iskeriot* in Nazaret. He would not care if I were gone ..."

Marta jabbed her finger accusingly at Yosef, "and now you can stand there and tell me that *I* would be abandoning them if I stayed here, if I got sick and untouchable, like you?"

Yosef blinked.

"Ah," she then remarked condescendingly, having realised something, "so now you have to admit, as to how with your love, your choices, your ending up here in this hell-hole, you yourself betrayed all those who loved you. Answer that one for me!"

Yosef could not. His heart sank as he looked away from her.

Marta took a tentative step forward. She reached out to him. "Yosef, I want to care for you—that is why I want to stay. I have no choice. I don't care whether it is a sin or not, whether I die or not. God only knows how many times I tried to kill my love for you."

Her voice fell, but Yosef could still make out the next words clearly.

"But ... but don't you see, love can never really be killed: it can only be buried, alive."

She took a couple of further steps towards him, then stopped abruptly in her tracks as Yosef, in a fit of fury, suddenly tore his clothes off and stood trembling and stark naked in front of her.

She instinctively shot her hands to her face and looked away.

Marta backed off, almost stumbling.

"Stop right there! Stop and look at me!" he yelled at her.

She hesitatingly lowered her hands and turned her face back to him, chest heaving. Marta gasped and trembled at the sight.

His frame was now bent like an old man's. He was much thinner, and each and every rib was visible through taut, dry, parchment-like skin. Every joint was swollen—elbows, knees. His yellowish skin was covered in patches and blisters of red and grey. And he was missing several toes and fingers.

"Marta, look at me. Do you think I want you to become like this?" he asked, his voice gentle and plaintive as he pointed with his gnarled and twisted fingers to his sunken chest. "Do you honestly think seeing you become like this will make me happy, will comfort me?"

The woman fell to a heap on the ground and sobbed heavily. Then she shuddered, and gazed at the ground, lost in thought.

Yosef looked at her mournfully. He remembered with great sadness the admiring looks she used to give him at his workshop. *Was that what was going through her head? How he was; what he has now been reduced to?*

"Hey, Marta," he finally said in an encouraging tone.

"Come on, get up now! Go back. Do not worry. My disease is far advanced. I shall not suffer much longer."

"You shall die soon?" she sobbed.

"Yes!" he replied grimly.

"So you won't have to love anymore?" she asked hopefully.

"I suppose not." He smiled, and added solemnly,

"Most men are remembered by what they achieved in their lives. Maybe some are meant to be remembered by what they endured."

He then started putting his clothing back on.

Yosef looked in wonder at her stunning, green, almond-shaped eyes; then gave her a sullen nod and held out a disfigured arm.

She held her arm out towards him. The distance between them seemed to shrink and he could swear they almost touched.

After some moments he dropped his arm, turned and hobbled back.

Marta watched with her arm still held out to him until he disappeared from view. Then, she dropped it suddenly and, head heaving on her chest, slowly made her way back to her mule.

YOSEF AND MARYAM

CHAPTER THIRTY THREE

The six Lepers strained and grunted as, hobbling, they carried the heavy bed over the rough path towards the post. They were followed by a second group of six men, who replaced them halfway there. After they had reached the spot, next to the fig tree where the donkey had been previously tethered, they laid it gently on the ground and huddled back to sit a safe distance away and downwind from it.

Not that there was much wind that night. Azaryahu had paced his way there before them under the dark sky, in which the stars had seemed exceptionally bright, even for a moonless night.

He now watched as the two visitors, a man and a woman, crossed beyond the circle of stones, and approached the spot where the bed lay. It was quite close to the settlement, yet for once, Azaryahu made no attempt to stop them. It was, after all, at the man's own, insistent, request.

The visitors came to the low bed and knelt down beside it. At the top of it, a donkey was also kneeling very close, with its head right over that of the occupant.

Under a rough blanket, Yosef was curled up on his side like a child, breathing raggedly. They touched him and he turned his face to look up. With a grunt and a huge effort he shifted onto his back.

He tried to raise his arms and speak but this exacerbated his breathing, and he dropped them back to his side with a cough and a wheeze.

The woman put a delicate finger to her lips. She laid her soft hand on his arm, and gripped it firmly. He gave up trying to move or speak and just braved a smile up at her.

"Yosef, have you heard of Yohanan, Zechariah's son?" she asked him.

Although he was now stone deaf, through his drooping eyelids, Yosef read the question from the slow and deliberate movements of her lips, and nodded his assent.

She then pointed to the man opposite her, who was intently gazing down at him.

"Tomorrow he is going to Yohanan, to the River Yarden, in order to be baptised by him."

Yosef smiled, nodded, and then coughed heavily again. Blood trickled down one side of his mouth and the woman wiped it away gently with her scarf.

She then turned and said something to the man. Yosef could just make out the question.

"My son, can you do something for him?"

Yosef blinked, and he chose not to read the reply.

So, head trembling, he averted his gaze.

"Woman, my hour is not yet come!" Yeshua's voice was strident.

Two tears welled up in Maryam's red-rimmed eyes, and they slowly inched their way like tiny pearls down her flushed cheeks.

She lowered her head.

Yosef continued his heavy breathing for a while. Then Yeshua placed a palm on his burning forehead.

Yosef's breathing relaxed. He turned and stared deeply into Yeshua's eyes. His own eyes then suddenly lit up brightly as they finally saw and understood.

Yosef inhaled his last breath, was first enveloped by darkness, *and then by light.*

And Yeshua wept.

EPILOGUE

And when Jesus was in Gadara at the house of Simon the Leper ...
[Matthew 26: (6-13)]

YOSEF AND MARYAM

AUTHOR BIOGRAPHY

Martin Baron, was born and brought up on the Mediterranean Island of Malta. Upon his graduation in Business Management in the mid-eighties, he took up the post of Manager for Libya with the national airline company.

He then set up his own business in the Travel sector, then in the Financial Services. He now owns and runs a restaurant in Valletta, Malta's capital. He has two daughters Kristina and Lara.

He has always had a keen interest in religion and scripture. Although he passed through a phase lasting many years as a self-proclaimed Atheist, he has long since fervently re-embraced Christianity.

Martin Baron's perennial quest for Truth makes him devote much of his time researching the paranormal, as well as religious, scientific and archaeological controversy.

He speaks several languages and as an adventurer, he has travelled the Globe extensively.

When he is not on the dance-floor, he enjoys a wide range of activities related to the sea.

He has written several poems, many of which he makes available on his Facebook page.
One of these was once chosen to be broadcast on BBC world radio.

Martin Baron is also a member of Mensa.

MARTIN BARON

YOSEF AND MARYAM

www.ingramcontent.com/pod-product-compliance
Lightning Source LLC
LaVergne TN
LVHW051510080426
835509LV00017B/2007